THOMAS COOK
Travellers

CYPRUS

Produced by AA Publishing

Written by Robert Bulmer

Series adviser: Melissa Shales

Edited, designed and produced by AA Publishing. Maps © The Automobile Association 1993

Distributed in the United Kingdom by AA Publishing, Fanum House, Basingstoke, Hampshire, RG21 2EA.

The contents of this publication are believed correct at the time of printing. Nevertheless, the publishers cannot accept responsibility for errors or omissions, or for changes in details given. Assessments of attractions, hotels, restaurants and so forth are based upon the author's own experience and, therefore, descriptions given in this guide necessarily contain an element of subjective opinion which may not reflect the publishers' opinion or dictate a reader's own experiences on another occasion.

We have tried to ensure accuracy in this guide, but things do change and we would be grateful if readers would advise us of any inaccuracies they may encounter.

A CIP catalogue record for this book is available from the British Library.

ISBN 0 7495 0624 5

Published by The Automobile Association and the Thomas Cook Group Ltd.

This book was produced using QuarkXPress™, Aldus Freehand™ and Microsoft Word™ on Apple Macintosh™ computers.

Colour separation: BTB Colour Reproduction, Whitchurch, Hampshire

Printed by Edicoes ASA, Oporto, Portugal

Cover Picture: *Paphos*
Title page: *Khrysokhou Bay near the Baths of Aphrodite*
Above: *Lefkara*

Contents

Introduction	4
History	6
Geography	8
Politics	10
Culture	12
Finding Your Feet	14
Walks	24
What to See	44
Getting Away From it All	142
Shopping	152
Entertainment	156
Sport	160
Food and Drink	166
Hotel Information	172
Practical Guide	176
Index and acknowledgements	191

Features

The Border	18
Beach Life	68
Carnivals	76
Café Life	88
Greek Weddings	94
Conservation	102
Greek Orthodoxy and the Monasteries	108
Wildlife	116
Life in the North	128
Village Life	146

Maps

Cyprus locator	8
Cyprus	16
Border	18
Walk 1 Greek Nicosia 1	24
Walk 2 Greek Nicosia 2	26
Walk 3 North Nicosia	28
Walk 4 Larnaca	30
Walk 5 Ayia Napa	32
Walk 6 Limassol	34
Walk 7 Paphos	36
Walk 8 Akamas	38
Walk 9 Aspros Gorge	40
Walk 10 Troodos	42
Nicosia	45
Larnaca	58
Limassol	72
Kourion	80
Paphos	85
Kyrenia	120
Famagusta	123
Salamis	132

Introduction

*W*hen powerful geological forces formed the island of Cyprus in the warm waters of the Mediterranean they created two uniquely different mountain ranges separated by a remarkable flat plain and a splendid coastline of bays, inlets and beaches. Nature then took the opportunity offered to exploit these features to the full and this is most wonderfully demonstrated in the springtime, when the whole island is transformed by wild flowers into a blaze of colour.

Today Cyprus is in the hands of another powerful force, tourism. Holiday towns now exist where not long ago there was nothing but bushes and sand dunes. In some parts the change has been so rapid that visitors can now lose their way in once-familiar surroundings. The island has withstood these assaults to some extent, for people go back with intriguing regularity. In fact, although many things are different, others are exactly as before. It is still possible to go down Ledra Street in Nicosia and see the same shops with the same miscellany of goods spilling into the street as years before, or to turn and find a unique corner of Cyprus hardly changed at all.

The village of Moutoullas set in the volcanic rock of the Troodos Mountains

It may be that one might pay a little over the top for an ice cream in Ayia Napa or Limassol, but the outrageously generous hospitality of the Cypriot is certainly as it always was, and guests will be fed beyond reasonable comfort. Also the irrepressible desire to please is undiminished. This is an endearing trait but can lead to some interesting results when asking the way.

Fine new highways now connect the towns of Nicosia, Larnaca and Limassol. This is good news for the visitor in a hurry for it will cut the journey time by half and avoids being stuck behind the Coca Cola wagon. Unfortunately he will miss all the villages *en route*, with the old men playing *tavali* in the square, the donkeys piled high with straw, the women carrying baskets of eggs. Nevertheless, the villages are still there and a detour of a few miles brings one to an older Cyprus where life goes on as it always did.

Cyprus is now an island with something for everybody. Young (and not so young) sun worshippers and disco dancers pour into Limassol, Ayia Napa and Protaras, from all over Europe. They undoubtedly have the time of their lives, their evening can be long, and many go straight from the nightspots to the beaches, saving breakfast for midday. Other visitors find the quiet beaches of Khrysokhou Bay, the hills and valleys of the Troodos Mountains and the disputed lands of northern Cyprus, to their liking. Indeed, while the Greeks are struggling to conserve what remains of their coastline the Turks have a vast unspoilt territory.

Cyprus lies at a crossroads between East and West. Over the centuries it was subjected to a multitude of different cultures which eventually crystallised into Greek and Turkish. Unfortunately the two communities no longer live side by side – they are separated by a line that runs from coast to coast, and only visitors to the south have the privilege of crossing the divide.

The forebears of the Turks in the north came from Turkey in the 16th century. Their language is Turkish and their religion Moslem. Hopitality and friendliness are as traditional as in the south, although of a slightly lower key. Perhaps one day the difficulties between the two communities will be resolved, but for the moment the visitor can only sympathise and then go out and enjoy what may just turn out to be the holiday of a lifetime.

CYPRUS QUOTES

History in this island is almost too profuse. It gives me a sort of mental indigestion.
Robert Byron, *The Road to Oxiana*

How does my old acquaintance of this isle? Honey, you shall be well desired in Cyprus; I have found great love amongst them.
Othello, Act 2, scene 1

Nothing real could ever have happened here.
Colin Thubron on Kyrenia

Realising that they will never be a world power, the Cypriots have decided for being a world nuisance.
George Mikes, quoted in *The Times*, 1980

The people are generally strong and nimble, of great civility, hospitable to their neighbours, and exceedingly fond of strangers.
William Lithgow, *Rare Adventures and Painfull Peregrinations*, 1614 – 32

The Cyprus wine is as sweet as the lyre of the Muses.
Elizabeth Browning

History

Stone Age 7200–2500 BC
The first settlers came to Cyprus in Neolithic times, probably on rafts from Asia Minor. One of their largest settlements was Khirokitia where the ruins of their beehive-shaped houses are to be clearly seen today. Other sites include Kastros and Tenta.

Bronze Age 2500–1050 BC
Immigration from Anatolia and later from Mycenae. Apart from bronze implements and jewellery there was rapid development of a ceramics industry. Trade took place for the first time with the other countries of the eastern Mediterranean.

Iron Age 1050–325 BC
A time of cultural innovation and the building of new cities such as Salamis. Metallurgy flourished more than ever. Cypro-Geometric pottery developed featuring matt black decoration.

10th century BC
The Phoencians arrived from Tyre and subjugated the island.

8th century BC
Assyrian rule. Cyprus's kings payed tribute to the Assyrians but were left to exercise local authority.

7th century BC
Assyrian Empire collapsed with the Egyptians eventually assuming control in 570 BC.

545 BC
Cyprus submitted to Persian domination.

323 BC
Start of Hellenistic period. Alexander the Great's victory at Tyre allowed Cyprus to throw off the Persian yoke. Shortly after, the Ptolemies of Egypt captured Cyprus. With their Greek antecedents Cyprus soon became firmly based in Greek culture.

58 BC
Roman annexation. Their great legacy of public building is to be seen today with the Sanctuary of Apollo Hylates at Kourion and the Temple of Zeus at Salamis. Other impressive remains can be found at Nea Paphos and Soli.

AD 330
Division of the Holy Roman Empire (Byzantine period), Cyprus was now ruled from Constantinople. The Church of Cyprus became fully established. The island became prosperous reflecting the administrative reforms carried out by Justinian. Churches instead of temples were constructed.

AD 647
Arab attacks weakened Byzantine control and did great damage with the island being pillaged and its inhabitants massacred. These attacks continued intermittently for the next 300 years.

AD 750
The Byzantines reasserted their authority and 100 years later the second golden age of Byzantium commenced lasting another 300 years. During this period Emperor Phokas routed the Arabs and Cyprus was left in peace.

1191
A period of relative quiet was broken when Richard the Lion Heart was obliged by bad weather to make a landfall near Limassol. This lead to conflict and a successful battle with the island's ruler Isaac Comnenos. Richard, needing more crusade resources, sold Cyprus to the Knights Templar in 1192.

Equally short of money the Templars had second thoughts about what was proving to be a troublesome purchase and asked Richard to take the island back, which he did to some financial advantage. Lion Heart then passed the island to a crusading Frankish knight, Guy de Lusignan.

1192–1489

Lusignan rule. The Lusignans ruled for nearly 300 years, operating a feudal system that was more admired outside than from within. After the death of Peter I in 1369 there was a steady decline in Frankish authority. The Genoese invaded the island, seizing Famagusta. Venetian help was used to drive out the invaders, but the liberators promptly took the opportunity of annexing the island for themselves in 1489.

1489–1571

Venetian rule. This is a period noted for persecution of the Greek Church. With the threat of Ottoman invasion, the Venetians constructed massive defences. Famagusta and Nicosia were encircled by the walls and bastions which still survive today. It was all to no effect, for a vast army of Turks stormed into Nicosia in 1570 and Famagusta surrendered in 1571.

1571–1878

Turkish rule. The island was settled by the Turks, creating two communities. Surprisingly, it was a period when the Greek Orthodox Church rose again and the archbishop acquired much power. In 1878, under the terms of an alliance, Turkey ceded the island to Great Britain for administrative and defence purposes, though it remained under the authority of the sultan. When Turkey entered World War I on Germany's side in 1914, Cyprus was formally annexed to Great Britain. In 1923 Turkey renounced any claim to the island.

1878–1960

British rule. As a British colony Cyprus prospered. However, problems emerged from the demands of many Greek Cypriots for unification with Greece (Enosis). This not only led to conflict with the British but also with the minority Turkish Cypriot community. In April 1955 a group of terrorists under the leadership of Colonel George Grivas pursued a terror campaign throughout Cyprus. By 1959 negotiations were held which led to an independence agreement. The Treaty of Zurich was signed in which Britain, Greece and Turkey guaranteed the independence of the new republic.

1960

Independence, with Archbishop Makarios becoming president. Hostilities between the communities flared up in 1963, resulting in the Turkish Cypriots eventually retreating into enclaves. United Nations soldiers were sent to Cyprus in the following year to keep the peace and they have been there ever since. In 1967 hostilities between the communities were renewed. National Organisation of Cypriot Combatants, EOKA, recommenced its campaign for Enosis.

1974

Coup and Turkish invasion. EOKA, with the support of the Greek military junta, carried out a coup against Makarios in July 1974 and appointed Nicos Sampson as president. This led to the invasion by Turkish forces five days later who took control of northern Cyprus. Talks failed to resolve the situation and in 1983 the Turkish Cypriots unilaterally declared the independence of northern Cyprus.

Geography

*I*n a sea full of islands, Cyprus is one of the more substantial ones. It is the third largest in the Mediterranean after Sardinia and Sicily, but is still only 240km long and 96km wide. A large central plain has mountains to north and south, and there is a varied coastline.

Its situation at the far eastern end of the Mediterranean, part of the Middle East but detached from it, is vital to understanding the nature and history of Cyprus. By virtue of its position the island has long been of great strategic importance, and any power with an interest in the Middle East has also had an interest in Cyprus.

While the island's culture, language and people are clearly Greek, the island is physically much closer to the Muslim world. Turkey is only 69km away; Syria 95km distant; while Athens lies at a distance of 800km.

Geology

The geological origins of Cyprus are still open to debate, but most current theories propose the view that the island was formed by some kind of volcanic explosion; this is definitely true of the Troodos Mountains, which are made of volcanic plutonic rock thrust up by the action of continental plates in prehistory.

The initial geological instability meant that Cyprus suffered from frequent earthquakes during its early history. Many of the prehistoric sites on the south coast were badly damaged by such quakes. The last one of significance was 50 years ago.

Mountains

The island is dominated by two mountain ranges; the Troodos and the Kyrenia (Besparmak). The former range is the highest, with Mount Olympus rising to more than 2,000m. This altitude ensures snow-cover through much of the winter. The higher slopes of the range are covered in pine and oak trees, but even on quite high and steep slopes there are extensive vineyards.

The height of the mountains means that even in summer the temperature is much lower than on the plain below. While the summer sees little rainfall, the winter rains and the melting snow are a vital resource and the visitor will notice many dams in the area.

The Troodos are also the source of many of Cyprus's minerals. Copper has been mined here since 3000 BC and may be the source of the island's name, Kypros in Greek.

The mountains descend gently towards Limassol and the southern coast. There is extensive cultivation of the lower slopes. In total contrast, the northern slopes in the Polis area can come down to the sea in spectacularly steep fashion.

The mountains of the Kyrenia range are about half as high as the Troodos but can be more impressive due to their craggy outline. Most notable is Mount Pentadaktylos (Besparmak in Turkish) which means five fingers, after the resemblance the peak has to five stumpy fingers. The range is made of sedimentary rocks forced up by pressure from movement of the continental plates.

There has been extensive deforestation of all the mountains, originally to provide wood to build the fleets of distant monarchs, including Alexander the Great, but also because of over grazing. The forestry department now works to reverse that trend and there are several extensive forests, especially in the west of the Troodos.

The Coast and the Plains

The coastline is extremely varied, and ranges from inaccessible rocky coves to extensive sandy beaches. There are two natural harbours at Limassol and Famagusta (Gazimagusa), and Larnaca has its own man-made port.

In between the two mountain ranges is the Mesaoria Plain, also known as the central plain, on which the island's capital Nicosia can be found. It is relatively fertile, incredible as this may seem at the end of summer when it resembles a dustbowl.

The main agricultural activity takes place in spring; the wheat is harvested at Easter. After that the lack of water takes its toll and all the rivers dry up.

In the far east is the narrow jutting segment of land known as the Karpas, also called the pan handle for obvious

reasons. This is an extremely remote area which has never been developed and seems unlikely to be exploited now that it is within the Turkish section of the island.

Windmills pump water to irrigate Cyprus's fertile plains

The Economy

Despite the lack of water – it rarely rains between April and October – one of the mainstays of the Cyprus economy is agriculture. In the east, windmills are employed to pump irrigation water on to the potato crops grown in the distinctive red soils of that region. Around Limassol and in the north near Guzelyurt (Morphou) are extensive citrus groves, and there are vineyards virtually everywhere.

Tourism is now the main source of income for the island. There are 1.5 million visitors each year and nearly every Cypriot has some interest in the industry, making the debate as to how much more development the island can sustain a particularly difficult one.

Politics

*P*olitics is never far from the surface in Cyprus. And it is little wonder; the struggle for Enosis (union with Greece) in the 1950s touched on every member of the community, and the compromise solution of independence in 1960 failed to provide the stability expected. For various reasons the constitution did not work well and the difficulties led to fighting between Greek and Turkish Cypriots, culminating in the present division of the island with the Turkish Cypriots holding the northern sector.

As the Greek Cypriot administration, and most of the world, does not recognise the division, the government is ostensibly as set up in 1960.

Statue of president Makarios, at the Archbishop's Palace in Nicosia

The president is the executive head of the government and is elected for a five-year term. The election takes place in two rounds, with candidates eliminated after the first round leaving the two leading candidates who must then gain over 50 per cent of the vote.

There is a council of ministers chosen from the House of Representatives. The members of the house are elected for five years. Under the constitution it was supposed to have 56 Greek Cypriot members and 24 Turkish Cypriot members. However, this agreement broke down in 1964 and since then it has functioned with only the 56 Greek Cypriot members.

In the north, the Turkish Cypriots unilaterally declared themselves independent in 1983. They have set up a government of 50 democratically elected members. Ten of these sit in the cabinet. There is a president and a prime minister, the former elected by the people, the latter appointed by the president. He usually nominates the chairman of the party with most seats. Currently this is the National Unity party. There are four other parties of various political persuasions, including the far left. Elections are held every four years.

In the south there are four main parties: Akel, the Communist party; EDEK, the Socialist party; the Democratic party, which is a centre party; and Democratic Rally, a party of the right.

The first presidential elections were won by Archbishop Makarios, the leader of the Church in Cyprus. He remained president until his death in 1977.

Despite the strength of the Communist party, Cyprus is an unashamedly free-market country with the only state owned industries being the public utilities.

Among the Greek Cypriots the debate is endless about how to reach an agreement with the Turkish Cypriot community and regain the lost lands.

It is a problem that has proved intractable. Newspaper headlines today are little different to those of the earliest days of the 'troubles'. They talk of hopes that are never fulfilled, for the Turks have little intention of changing the clock back to 1974.

Nevertheless, these days Cyprus, or it should be said southern Cyprus, is one of the wealthiest countries in the Middle East. The setback of 1974 has been substantially overcome. Unemployment is now down to 2 per cent and since 1975 the GDP has grown to 6 per cent.

Visitors will see evidence of this in the major infrastructure projects being undertaken by the government, ranging from new roads to dams.

Cyprus has a good public education system which is compulsory from the age of 5 $\frac{1}{2}$. Children attend primary school until the age of 11 and then go to the gymnasium. After three years there is division between academic education and more technical subjects. The University of Cyprus is due to open in 1992–3.

The health service is free only to those on low incomes. However, the health of the nation is very good, with average life expectancy 78 for women and 74 for men.

In the south, government services have focused strongly on helping the refugees from the north who initially placed heavy burdens, particularly on housing provision, and visitors will see new settlements built for them.

Despite everything, Cyprus must be one of the most stable countries in the region with the democratic tradition fairly well entrenched, although as was seen during the coup of 1974, with a certain potential for volatility.

Culture

*C*yprus, perhaps not surprisingly given its small size, has not had any great impact on international culture. Furthermore the few home-grown artists have tended to move abroad; not that this prevents the Cypriots claiming and celebrating them as their own.

Zeno, the Stoic philosopher, was one such. He was born in Larnaca and is much celebrated there. But he left the island at an early age and his Stoic philosophy of grinning and bearing the injustices of life, was worked out in the intellectual hothouse of Athens.

Petra Tou Romiou, Aphrodite's birth place

Cyprus in Mythology

Cyprus's culture is inextricably linked to its history and its place in early Greek mythology. Most impressively, the island is reputed to have been the birthplace of Aphrodite. She emerged from the waves at Petra tou Romiou which is still a spectacular spot and that birth has inspired numerous painters all over the world. The most famous painting to result is Botticelli's *Birth of Venus*, where she is depicted emerging from the sea upon a seashell.

Aphrodite kept a long-standing connection with the island and found several of her many lovers here, ranging from Akamas to Adonis. Her influence persists through the hundreds of cafés and restaurants which have been named after her.

Further flattering references appear in Homer's *The Odyssey*, which confirms Aphrodite's presence on the island with the line 'Paphos, in Cyprus has her precinct and fragrant altar'. Visitors today can visit the Baths of Aphrodite near Polis where legend has it the goddess bathed after a night of passion.

Cultural History

The Romans had little cultural impact except perhaps through their buildings; the best examples being the theatres at Salamis and Kourion.

The Lusignans, however, left a considerable legacy of fine buildings in Gothic style and brought considerable Italian and western European influence to the island.

Yet it was in the Byzantine period that Cyprus really flowered into a major cultural centre through the single medium of icon painting in the churches across the island. These paintings, many of which are well preserved, are among the finest examples in the Mediterranean.

Some of the best icon painters in Europe came to practise their art, such as Philip Goul, who decorated the churches of Stavros tou Ayiasmati and Ayios Mamas at Louvaras.

The effort which went into painting literally hundreds of churches is quite extraordinary and has left a remarkable legacy.

The Turkish period seems to have seen a decline in cultural activity which has persisted ever since. However, there is a strong folk culture with a long tradition.

The dying art of silversmiths can be seen today at craft centres

Folk Art

There is a rich heritage of old folk ballads and poems which have been passed on from generation to generation and which are now recited at festivals and village fairs. The folk music and dances have followed a similar pattern, although tend only to be seen in the contrived displays put on for tourists.

There are other more tangible manifestations of folk art in pottery and jewellery. Weaving, crochet and lace-making are still very much part of the lives of Cypriot women, especially in the villages. Fine examples of intricately sewn national costumes can be seen in the folk museums across the island. Lefkara, a village in the hills east of Limassol, is the home of lace-making. The craft could date back to the Assyrian period since early lace has been found at Salamis. However, Cypriot lace did not gain international recognition until the 15th century when Leonardo da Vinci bought a consignment of Lefkara lace to decorate Milan Cathedral.

Cypriot copper and silversmiths also had an international reputation and can still be seen at work in some of the handicraft centres, but the art is dying out today.

Overall, Cyprus is a strange mixture of cultures. This stems from its history. From the 16th century it has had a Turkish minority which grew to more than 25 per cent of the population; hence the profusion of mosques in all the main towns. Then there are various refugees from around the Mediterranean, most notably the Armenians and in recent years the Lebanese, all of whom have had an influence on Cypriot culture.

However, what will be most striking to the visitor will be the legacy of the British colonial period. Western culture, theatre and films are all well received here, not least because English is so well understood.

In the middle of all this is the influence of Greece: both of classical Greece from where so many settlers came and modern Greece which provides the pop songs of contemporary Cyprus. Cypriot culture itself remains elusive, a curious mixture of styles which adapts to suit what it thinks its audience wants to hear. This is the secret of the island's charm and also its most irritating quality.

Finding your feet

*T*he first thing to strike a first-time summer visitor to Cyprus will be the heat; stepping off the plane can seem like walking into the blast of hot air from a hairdryer. The second and not unrelated experience will be that of thirst. Visitors are likely to drink three times as much as at home, not out of a desire to over indulge but out of a genuine thirst. As a result, do not expect, in summer, to be able to undertake any strenuous exercise while on holiday; do not be concerned if a five-minute walk at midday prompts a feeling of exhaustion.

Arrival

Expect chaos at the airport. The buildings are too small and the holiday flights tend to arrive all at once.

Huge numbers of taxis gather at the airport; usually distinctive elongated Mercedes with worry beads hanging from the front mirror. These drivers believe speed is of the essence and are masters of the art of finely judged overtaking.

Driving

For those preferring to trust their own driving skills, there is a multitude of car hire firms at the airport and all around the resorts. Car hire is expensive, but reasonable deals can be struck with local firms. Check that the price includes collision damage waiver (to avoid being responsible for the first £500 of damage) and check the condition of vehicle, especially the tyres, before departing (see page 179).

Driving is on the left. The roads are generally good and well signposted. The new dual carriageways which link Larnaca and Limassol to Nicosia make crossing the island much more rapid. There are however, still many stretches of single carriageway where very slow-moving lorries can be encountered.

The towns can be very busy especially in the evening rush hour and visitors should remember that Cypriot drivers have a cavalier attitude to the highway code.

Where to Stay

Cyprus is well set up for the tourist and many of the new hotels are of a very high quality.

The independent traveller can get by, although not as cheaply as might be expected. The idea of rooms to rent is beginning to spread to Cyprus but only to a very limited extent. At the moment it is concentrated in the west of the island and in some of the medium- sized villages. Otherwise, the independent

Car and bike hire is available for those visitors who wish mobility

Traffic congestion in Limassol at peak times can be a problem

Mosquitoes

While mosquitoes in Cyprus do not carry malaria they can still be a real pest. They are less prevalent on the coast than inland. Visitors should ensure they have insect repellent and mosquito coils. Protect wrists and ankles in the evening and make sure the room is clear before going to bed.

traveller can take their chance with the hotels or confine themselves to the campsites (see page 172).

Mountains

All visitors who want to gain a complete picture of Cyprus should spend some time in the mountains. The Troodos Mountains are particularly high and provide a welcome escape from the heat of the plains. There are several hill resorts with good hotels and restaurants and plenty to do, from walking to exploring the Byzantine churches. With their labyrinthine streets, the mountain villages tumbling down the hillside have a distinctive charm worth savouring.

In winter visitors can enjoy the rare pleasure of a Mediterranean skiing holiday. There is usually snow on Mount Olympus from December to March.

The Coast

The coastline of Cyprus is extremely varied. The southeast of the island, around Ayia Napa, has grown into one of the major tourist resorts, catering especially for young people. It has lost much of its Cypriot character and the profusion of discos may not appeal to everyone. There are certainly some of the best sandy beaches in this area, but unfortunately they have now become very crowded. The beaches around Limassol and Larnaca are longer and although they have extensive development they offer more room to move. Avoid the beaches in town.

The towns of Limassol and Larnaca themselves now cater for the tourist trade but started out as industrial centres.

The region between Limassol and

Paphos has more sites of interest per kilometre than any other part of the island: the medieval castle of Kolossi to the grand theatre of Kourion, taking in the ancient site of Palea

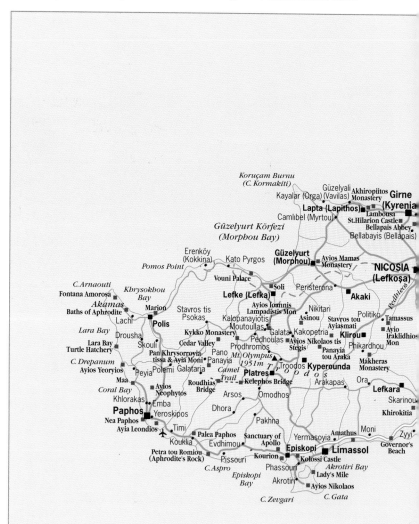

Paphos, embraces some of the most important archaeological finds in the Mediterranean. An added bonus to a trip round this area are the fine beaches.

The main road passes some distinctive white cliffs with glorious photographic opportunities at Petra tou Romiou, where Aphrodite is supposed to have sprung from the waves.

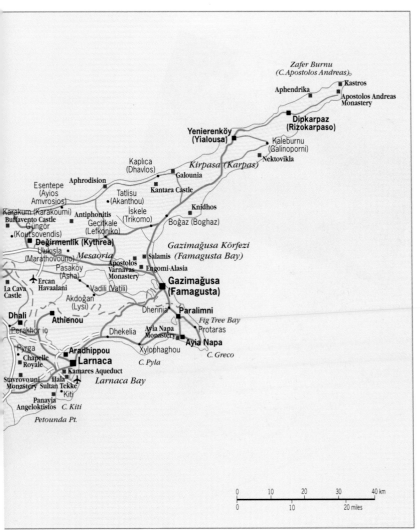

The Border

Green Line

The description 'Green Line' dates from the troubles of 1963 when Nicosia was partitioned. A British intermediary drew a line on a map of the city and it was in green ink. Now it is used to describe the line in its island-wide entirety.

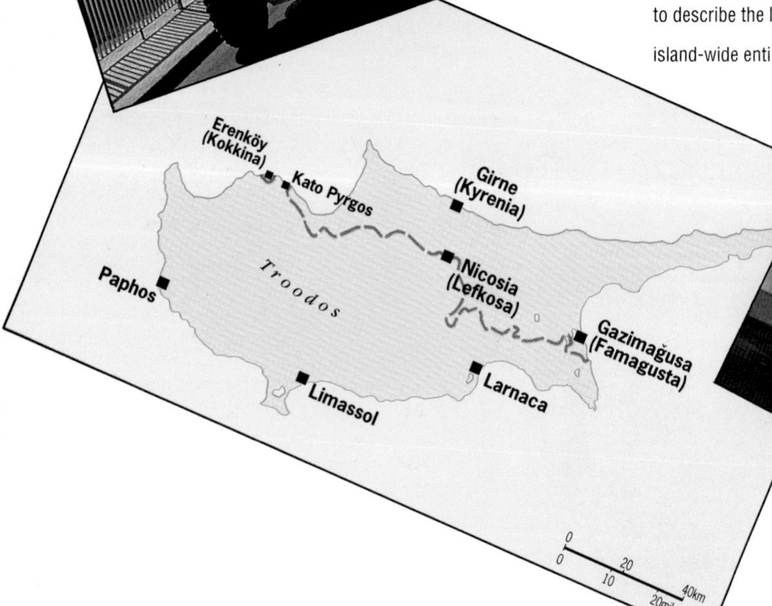

Erenköy
(Kokkina)

Kato Pyrgos

Girne
(Kyrenia)

Paphos

Troodos

Nicosia
(Lefkosa)

Gazimağusa
(Famagusta)

Limassol

Larnaca

0
0   20   40km
    10   20miles

People not familiar with Cyprus's troubles can be shocked at the first sighting of United Nations soldiers. The soldiers are likely to be taking their leave in the bars and cafés of the resorts, apparently on holiday themselves. Nevertheless, they are there on serious business, mainly to keep the peace between Greek and Turkish Cypriots. They first came in 1964 when the Turks retreated into enclaves for safety. Since 1974 they have had a much bigger task, for the division now runs from Pyrgos in the west to Famagusta in the east, passing through the centre of old Nicosia. There are observation posts along the entire 200km border where Greeks in the south face Turks in the north. The no man's land is held by the United Nations.

In Nicosia's ancient walled town Greeks and Turks can see the whites of each others' eyes. In the aftermath of the 1974 fighting this was not a friendly confrontation, and every once in a while the night sky would explode into a firework display of tracer shells down the length of the line. Today it is different, the advancing years have drawn the sting of anger and hatred. A surreptitious trade is carried on: it could be cigarettes for the Greeks, whisky for the Turks; even so, tricks are played and rifleman Osman Pasha might just find that his whisky tastes a little like cold tea!

The line is a serious obstacle to anybody wishing to see the whole island. Visitors to the north cannot cross it, while visitors in the south can go to the north for one day at a time, but they have to be back by 5.30pm.

The only crossing point is in Nicosia by the old Ledra Palace Hotel. Visitors will know when they are there as sandbags and buildings pockmarked by bullets put a disconcerting tension into the air.

A Greek policeman will check passports and perhaps point to notices asking people not to go. At the Turkish checkpoint there are forms to fill in, a pound to pay, and a required statement that the visitor recognises the Turkish Cypriot state. Unlike the rest of Cyprus, little has changed here since 1974.

Paphos and the West

Paphos is growing rapidly into a tourist resort but it too has some very impressive archaeological sites such as the House of Dionysos and the Tombs of the Kings.

The far west of the island has the most remote and arguably the most beautiful areas. There is only one place of any size: Polis, which is the

The sea front and harbour at Paphos, a rapidly growing resort

backpackers paradise with rooms to rent everywhere and a campsite right on the beach. Beyond Polis to Pomos Point are long stretches of beach where there is not a hotel or other tourist in sight.

Nicosia

Nicosia, the island's capital, is a modern, sophisticated place, although within the walls, the atmosphere of the old town is preserved with narrow streets and dark shops.

Language

Many Cypriots speak very good English and although they will appreciate attempts to speak Greek, it is far from necessary. The Cypriot attempt at written English can however, be less than accurate.

Traditions are maintained in the old town Nicosia

The North

The north (Turkish Cyprus) has a very different atmosphere. It sees many fewer tourists and its sites are consequently much more peaceful. Northern Nicosia has the air of a Turkish bazaar; Kyrenia is a pleasant harbour with a fort at one end while Famagusta old town is one of the best-preserved Venetian towns in the Mediterranean. The new town lies empty and ghostly, inaccessible to all but the military since the invasion of 1974.

The Cypriot and the Tourist

The Cypriots make life easy for the tourist; they speak the same language as most visitors and their innate genial gregariousness makes the foreigner feel at ease. Cypriots are masters of the tourist industry, they remember your name and will go out of their way to be helpful.

The other side of this coin is, however, that they have no concept of privacy and their constant presence can at times be an irritation.

This is a particular problem for female visitors who may find the sexist attitudes of the older Cypriot male a little hard to stomach.

There is also a certain tension between the liberal morality of visitors and that to which the Cypriots, or at least the Cypriot Church, is trying to cling. Cypriot women still keep themselves to themselves and even younger women will refuse a harmless conversation with a foreign man.

Sunburn

Visitors should take care not to spend too long in the sun in their first days on the island. The sun is at its height between 11am and 3pm when less than 60 minutes can turn the white tourist blazing pink.

Street entertainment in Nicosia market

Cypriot Life

To an extent Cypriots are bemused by foreigners. They do not share the passion for sun, sand and sea; most Cypriots spend their holidays in the mountains. Their visits to the beach are limited to the very height of summer, at other times they claim it is too cold.

Cypriots seem happiest sitting in the café playing backgammon and discussing the intricacies of the political situation and whether the 'troubles' will ever be sorted out.

There is a strong enterprise culture; if it moves sell it to the tourists is a motto some seem to have adopted. Yet despite the aggressive salesmanship that can be encountered there is still a point at which even the desire to earn more money fades and the Cypriot likes to lie back and put things off until tomorrow.

The Daily Timetable

Business gets going earlier than visitors might be used to. Most offices are open by 8am. Then there is the siesta; that glorious peaceful period between 12 noon and 3pm in summer when the more sensible citizens are relaxing in the cool of their homes.

Things get going again around 4pm, and by 5pm it is pandemonium in most towns. Shops stay open until about 7pm and most Cypriots eat about 8pm or later, although restaurants are happy to serve you at any time of day. Despite their early start, Cypriots stay up late.

Expatriate Life

Living in Cyprus – and many expatriates do set up transitory residence here – is

The game Tivali may not always be a cooling antidote for the afternoon sun

on the one hand idyllic: the glorious days of summer, the relaxed way of doing things, the lack of crime and the way things are reassuringly similar to home. But it also has its drawbacks: the relaxed way of doing things means that delivery will be promised tomorrow and tomorrow will never come. The initial over-intimacy with local people may fade or remain frustratingly superficial and there are basic differences of culture which cannot be ignored in a long stay. And curious as it may sound, it is even possible to become tired of going to the beach every weekend.

As a result, the expatriate community tends to set up its own groups and amusements. Few have much to do with the itinerant tourists, and the long-stay residents even tend to socialise together rather than with those who are only there for a couple of years.

Greek Nicosia 1

This walk takes in the main shopping streets of Nicosia and some of the historical points of interest. *Allow 1 hour, longer if the Archaeological Museum is visited.*

Start at Laiki Yitonia just inside the city walls.

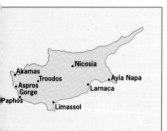

Nearby

British Council

Makarios III Avenue

1 LAIKI YITONIA

This area of the city has been restored very successfully to provide several pedestrianised streets of craft shops, traditional restaurants and the tourist office.
Turn on to Ippocratous Street, the main pedestrianised street of Laiki Yitonia, to find the Leventis Museum.

2 LEVENTIS MUSEUM

This is a new museum with exhibits which tell the history of Nicosia. By Cypriot standards it is a very sophisticated museum employing videos and other modern technology.

It has three floors of interest: the first floor covers the city's early history up until Turkish rule; the ground floor more recent history from British rule to independence; and there are some medieval artefacts in the basement.
Proceed towards Onasagoras Street and turn right. Continue into

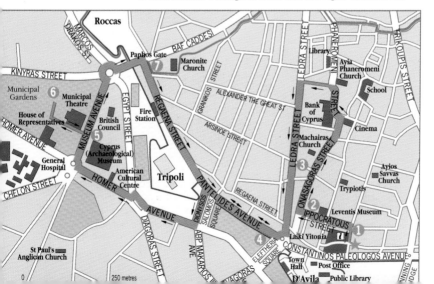

Phaneromeni Street and eventually reach Phaneromeni Church, supposedly the biggest in Nicosia. Turn left just before the church and then left again into Ledra Street.

Busy shoppers in Nicosia

3 LEDRA AND ONASAGORAS STREET

These two narrow streets were once the main shopping areas of Nicosia. They still attract large numbers of people to their bustling narrow pavements.

They are lined by a wide range of shops. The most notable are those selling cloth which is stacked in rolls outside the shops.

Continue to the top end of Ledra Street where it meets Eleftheria Square.

4 ELEFTHERIA SQUARE

This is a busy place lined with kiosks on one side and a bastion of the city walls on the other. It is very much the heart of the city, standing as the gateway between the old and the new.

Turn right here to keep inside the city walls on Pantelides Avenue and then left in

Dionysos Solomos Square which serves as the main bus station. From here cross over the walls and turn right into Homer Avenue and then head straight on, passing the American Cultural Centre and the Cyprus Museum. At the second set of lights turn right into Museum Avenue. The museum entrance is on the right.

5 CYPRUS (ARCHAEOLOGICAL) MUSEUM

This houses one of the finest collections of archaeological treasures in the Mediterranean.

The first exhibits are objects from the Neolithic period, including a wall painting of a man with his hands up. Next comes the Bronze Age followed by artefacts from the classical Greek period. At the end of room 4 is perhaps the most impressive display: a whole case of steatite idols arranged as they were found in a sanctuary at Ayia Irini.

The remaining rooms pass through the various periods of history. Be sure not to miss the Salamis treasure in a room upstairs.

Turn right out of the museum and cross the road to the municipal theatre and gardens.

6 MUNICIPAL GARDENS

Well-watered gardens full of trees, flowers, a few ponds and a small collection of sad-looking birds.

Return to Museum Street and turn left to reach the roundabout at the bottom. Take the third exit, over which a UN flag flies.

7 PAPHOS GATE

This used to be one of the main gateways into the city through the walls but it has fallen into disrepair.

Turn uphill keeping close to the walls passing the fire station and eventually emerging back at Eleftheria Square.

Greek Nicosia 2

This walk explores the sights within the walls of the eastern part of the city. *Allow 1 hour, longer if you visit any of the museums.*

Start at Kanning Bridge, head into the old city down Tri-koupis Street, passing a shop on the corner which sells bags.

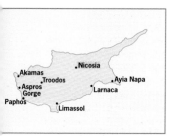

Nearby

Laiki Yitonia

Eleftheria Square

1 TRIKOUPIS STREET

Trikoupis Street is typical of the old city, narrow with even narrower pavements cluttered further by the overspill from shops and cafés. It is faintly shabby but has a certain charm. *On the right, after about 200m, the Omerye Mosque is reached.*

2 OMERYE MOSQUE

Originally a church, this building was converted into a mosque by the Turks to commemorate the Moslem prophet Omer, who was thought to have stayed here. It has a particularly large minaret. Today it is used for prayer by visiting Arabs. *Turn right into Tylliria Square and right again into Patriarchis Gregorios Street, and after 100m on the right is Hadjigeorgakis Kornessios House.*

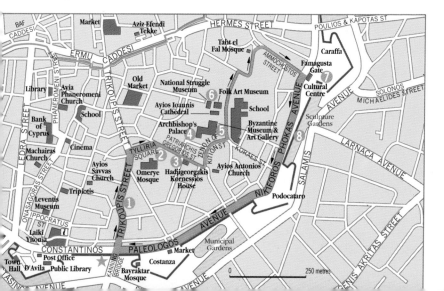

3 HADJIGEORGAKIS KORNESSIOS HOUSE

This was the home of Hadjigeorgakis, the official interpreter (dragoman) to the Turkish governor, a very prestigious position. The building has now been restored and turned into a museum.

The house is built around a courtyard and is a fine example of 18th-century Turkish architecture. The museum contains artefacts from the Turkish period (see page 48).

Turn left down Zenon of Kition Street to reach the Archbishop's Palace.

4 ARCHBISHOP'S PALACE

The archbishopric is a large mock-Venetian-style palace which is not open to the public. It is dominated by a huge black statue of Archbishop Makarios who was president of the island until his death in 1977.

Continue past the archbishopric to the adjacent cathedral and museums.

5 BYZANTINE MUSEUM AND AYIOS IOANNIS CATHEDRAL

In the courtyard behind the archbishopric various cultural projects have been undertaken including the establishment of a museum of Byzantine art. Housed in the cloisters at the back of the courtyard, the museum has a fine collection of 9th- to 18th-century icons.

Ayios Ioannis Cathedral was built in 1662 on the site of a Benedictine abbey. It has a fine display of restored paintings on the roof and walls. The archbishops of Cyprus are enthroned here.

There is also a folk art museum in one of the buildings behind the cathedral, containing traditional costumes, weaving looms and a wide range of tools.

Continue down the road.

6 NATIONAL STRUGGLE MUSEUM

This contains photographs and documents relating to the fight for independence from Britain. It is inevitably a rather partisan account.

Continue northwards and after a five-minute walk enter a pedestrianised area which is being restored. At the far end of the road is the Taht el Fal Mosque, not usually open to the public. Turn right on to Ammochostos Street and head for the Famagusta Gate at the far end.

Famagusta Gate, the finest Venetian monument in Nicosia

7 FAMAGUSTA GATE

This used to be one of the main entrances through the walls into the old city. Restored, it is now an art centre which holds cultural events.

Turn left to follow the walls.

8 VENETIAN WALLS

The walls are perhaps the most impressive sight in Nicosia and stretch for 4.5km with 11 bastions.

Follow the road round the walls, passing the football pitch, the Bayraktar Mosque on the bastion, and then returning to Kanning Bridge.

Northern Nicosia

For those staying in the southern side of the island this walk will give them an insight into the island's 'troubles' and into the different culture and perspective of Turkish Cyprus. Those on holiday in the north will find this a useful way of exploring northern Nicosia. *Allow 1 hour.*

Nearby

Arabahmet Mosque

Bedesten

New Market

Haidar Pasa Mosque

From Paphos Gate follow Marcos Dracos Avenue north to the checkpoint at the old Ledra Palace Hotel.

1 PASSING THROUGH THE CHECKPOINT

Tourists are currently allowed through the Ledra Palace checkpoint until 2pm and have to return by 5.30pm. There are various formalities to be completed for both the Greek and Turkish authorities.

Walk through the Greek checkpoint into the UN buffer zone, complete the formalities at the Turkish checkpoint then head straight on to the roundabout where you should turn right to follow the line of the city walls. Turn into the old city at Kyrenia (Girne) Gate.

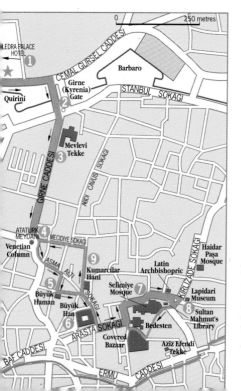

2 KYRENIA (GIRNE) GATE

This used to be one of three gateways into the old city, built by the Venetians. The Turks added to it but the British decided it was too narrow and built a new entrance, and the old gateway now stands rather strangely in the middle of the road while the traffic passes on either side.

Go into the city on Girne Caddesi and after 100m on the left is the Mevlevi Tekke.

3 MEVLEVI TEKKE

This 17th-century building was the home of the whirling Dervishes, a religious sect who gyrated in a distinctive dance on the stage. The building is now the Ethnographical Museum.

Continue down Girne Caddesi for a further
200m to reach Atatürk Square.

4 ATATÜRK MEYDANI (ATATÜRK SQUARE)

Atatürk was the founder of modern
Turkey and his statue can be found all
over northern Cyprus. In the centre of
the square is a much older monument, a
Venetian column. The tourist office and
Hotel Saray, the main hotel of northern
Nicosia, can be found here.

*Bear left with the road and then take the
first direct left, passing a furniture shop,
using the twin minarets of the Selimiye
Mosque as a landmark. Follow the first
right to reach the Turkish Bath.*

*Buvuk Haman, only the entrance of the
former church remains*

5 TURKISH BATH (BÜYÜK HAMAN)

This was originally a Christian church
(St George of the Latins) but was
converted to a Turkish Bath which is still
used today. The proprietor will show
you round; leading you from the cool of
the fountain house into progressively
hotter rooms. Those wishing to have a
bath may do so.

*Turn right out of the Bath, then right again
until the turrets of Büyük Han come into
view.*

6 BÜYÜK HAN

Built in 1572, Büyük Han was formerly
a Turkish inn with two storeys of rooms
and an octagonal mosque in the square.
It is being restored, and although
completion is still some way in the
future, visitors are already allowed
limited access. Check with the tourist
office.

*Cross the car park and turn right leading
into a pedestrian area. At the far end is the
Green Line. Turn left to the Selimiye
Mosque.*

7 SELIMIYE MOSQUE

This was originally the Santa Sophia
Cathedral, built in 1209, and was the
most imposing building in Nicosia. It is
now a mosque with high arches on huge
pillars and is still used for religious
services. Visitors can enter if they are
suitably dressed (see page 57).

   Behind the mosque are the sultan's
library and the Lapidari Museum.

8 LAPIDARY MUSEUM

The museum, in a 15th-century
Venetian house, has a display of holy
relics from the Selimiye Mosque and
other religious sites.

*Take the path round the left-hand side of
the mosque, passing the Bedesten which used
to be the market. Return to the pedestrian
area and take the first right. At the
crossroads is Kurmarcilar Hani.*

9 KUMARCILAR HANI

This again used to be an inn and now
has shops built into its walls. The owner
of the café will let you through to the
courtyard.

*Circle round the Khan and then take the
road to the north, Akiah Efendi Sokagi,
then left to reach Atatürk Square, some
100m further on.*

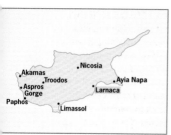

Larnaca

This walk explores the main tourist and shopping areas of Larnaca. *Allow 1 hour*

Start 100m inland from the fort at the Grand Mosque of Larnaca.

Nearby

Archaeological Museum

1 KEBIR MOSQUE

This is one of several mosques in this part of the town which used to be the Turkish area. It is still in use; the prayer times are posted up outside but it is open to suitably dressed visitors. *Head towards the seafront and the fort.*

2 LARNACA FORT

Built by the Turks as a fort in 1625, this structure has since been used as a prison and is now a museum with exhibits from the site of Kition. Visitors may wish to exploit its seafront position and refresh their feet in the lapping waters beyond the sea wall.

Head north from the fort, along the coastal road, passing the Megalos Pefkos and other similar cafés.

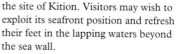

3 LARNACA BEACH

Larnaca's beach seems to attract many visitors despite its far-from-scenic aspect. It is man-made, the sand a green colour, and even with the best efforts of the authorities it tends to get dirty.

Either walk along the beach, if it is not too crowded, or keep to the coastal road. After about 200m, on the right of the road, opposite a small car park, is the statue of Kimon the Athenian.

4 KIMON THE ATHENIAN

Kimon was one of the greatest heroes of early Cypriot history. He led a fleet of 200 triremes against the Persians but was killed in the ensuing battle.

Those with troubles reputedly

consult the statue for advice.
*Continue along the road and turn right
towards the sea. Walk along the breakwater.*

*The bust of the great Athenian hero Kimon,
is reputed to give 'advice' to the troubled*

5 MARINA/SEA WALL

The marina is fenced off to all but those
who have boats moored here. However,
there is a pleasant walk along the
boulders of the breakwater which is also
a good place to swim from.
*Turn inland on a busy stretch of road to
Vasileos Pavlou Square where the tourist
office can be found. At Barclays Bank
turn left into Zinonos Kitieos Street and
after 100m on the right is the Pierides
Museum.*

6 PIERIDES MUSEUM

This 18th-century house with grey
shutters contains an extensive collection
of archaeological finds that once
belonged to Demetrios Pierides, a
Cypriot archaeologist.
Continue on this street.

7 ZINONOS KITIEOS STREET

This is the main shopping street in
Larnaca. The yellow building inland
from Chrysios dress shop is the
Armenian church and school. There is a
large Armenian community in Cyprus
which fled from Turkey in 1896.
*A confusing crossroads confronts the walker
at the end of Zinonos Kitieos Street. Care
should be taken as paving is poor to non-
existent. Go straight, then take a sharp right
and follow the road round to the left. Pass a
mosque with a stumpy truncated minaret
which is now the youth hostel. Turn right
into Dionysos Street to see Ayios Lazaros
Church directly ahead.*

8 AYIOS LAZAROS CHURCH

Built in the 9th century, the church has a
distinctive white-painted belfry. It
commemorates Lazaros, who, having
been raised from the dead arrived in
Cyprus and became Bishop of Larnaca.
The church is surrounded by
peaceful cloisters, and is closed between
12 noon and 3pm in summer.
*Proceed towards Dionysos Street, but take
the first right followed by the first left to
return to the fort and seafront.*

*Ayios Lazaros church in Larnaca is
surrounded by peaceful cloisters*

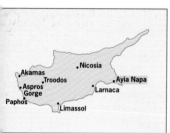

Ayia Napa

Ayia Napa has developed into one of the most popular tourist resorts. This walk explores parts of that area but also the more peaceful region along the coast. *Allow 2 hours.*

Start at the village square.

Nearby

White Cliffs

Nissi Beach

1 AYIA NAPA SQUARE

The large square in front of the monastery is a pleasant place to sit. At night there are stalls selling copper goods and jewellery. Towards the end of the summer, during the Ayia Napa festival, music and dance displays take place in the square.
Enter the monastery courtyard.

2 AYIA NAPA MONASTERY

The monastery is by far the most impressive sight in Ayia Napa. It is a green and peaceful place, now used as a conference centre.

The monastery was supposedly founded by a Venetian noblewoman on the site of a cave where an icon of the Virgin Mary had been found. The building was restored in 1950.
Pass through the monastery courtyard and out through an archway on to a path. There is a pool on the right where frogs and cicadas sing at night. Below is a huge new church. The path leads on to a tarred

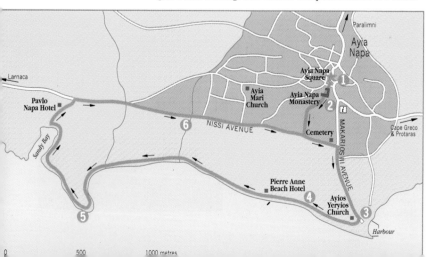

road heading to the sea. When it meets the main coast road, turn left to reach a small cemetery and then right to the harbour.

3 HARBOUR

The harbour retains its character despite the building going on around it. Small fishing boats are moored here and some larger tourist ships take visitors on cruises to the surrounding area. The long beach is fine and sandy, although it can become crowded with residents from nearby hotels.

Take the path to the right of the small church, passing some houses built around a courtyard.

4 AGRICULTURE

Notice the red soil in this area. Its high fertility supports the region's extensive potato crop. In the distance the visitor will hear the motor of the water pumps, so essential to a successful crop. Many of these are driven by steel windmills, one of which is visible in the distance from the path.

Walk across the scrubland. There is a small beach to the left and after about 200m, the path reaches the Pierre Anne Beach Hotel. Follow the track at its far end, skirting the swimming pool and head towards the sea.

Continue on the track, the sea is accessible but the shoreline very rocky. The track now enters a ditch. Cross this maintaining the new building on the right-hand side and skirt round a bamboo grove keeping close to the sea. Emerge on to a beach with sun-beds. (This is a $^1/_2$ hour walk from the harbour.) The beach improves as the walker heads west.

Take the track which rises gently on to the headland.

5 HEADLAND

From here there are wonderful views:

The walk by Ayia Napa harbour is lined by many restaurants

to the east lies Cape Greco; to the west, a stretch of rocky coast, and in the distance, the far promontory of Nissi Beach. The headland has the typical spiky rocks of the area.

From the headland walk on the track which bears left and leads suddenly into a sandy cove, once known as Sandy Bay. Walkers can return the way they have come or head through the grounds of the Pavlo Napa Hotel to the main road, Nissi Avenue. There is a footpath on the right-hand side of the road.

6 NISSI AVENUE

The route passes the Kallenos apartments on the left, covered in bright purple bougainvillaea in late summer, while on the right are windmills and agricultural land. This does not last, however, and the road soon acquires all the tourist trappings of shops and cafés.

After 0.5km Makarios III Avenue is reached. Turn right to regain the harbour area.

Limassol

Limassol is one of the principal industrial and commercial centres of the island. This walk explores the main sites of interest and shopping districts of the town. *Allow 1 hour, longer if you visit the castle.*

Begin from the car park on the seafront almost opposite the Limassol Palace Hotel.

Nearby

Archaeological Museum

1 SEAFRONT

Although there is no beach, the seafront is wide and palm lined. Off shore there is almost always a long queue of ships waiting to enter the new port at the far west of the city. *Initially, take the disused road nearest the sea to avoid the traffic on the main thoroughfare. Then after 5 minutes walking move inland to join the main road and pass several shops selling pottery and copper goods. Continue past the tourist office to a roundabout and turn left towards the old harbour.*

2 HARBOUR

This is the old harbour now serving only pleasure and fishing boats. The new port is several kilometres to the west. In the early morning, fishermen land their catch here and set up stalls to sell it.

A new attraction has emerged by the harbour; a much-advertised reptile house, containing cobras and crocodiles among the highlights. The rather sad-looking caged monkey outside is something of a deterrent.

The city of Limassol can be observed from the battlements of its castle

Turn right at the roundabout to the castle opposite the Kasti coffee shop, on the left-hand side of the road.

3 LIMASSOL CASTLE AND MEDIEVAL MUSEUM

Lying in pleasant grounds the current building was constructed in the 14th century. Richard the Lion Heart married Berengaria in the castle chapel (no longer visible).

The castle now houses a fine medieval museum with three levels. In the dungeon are artefacts from Byzantine churches, on the ground floor is a wide range of tombstones, paintings and pottery, and on the second floor are some very impressive suits of armour. It is also possible to climb right up to the battlements and look out over the city.

On leaving the castle, take the first road to the right and 100m away is the grand mosque of Limassol.

4 GRAND MOSQUE OF LIMASSOL

This mosque is still in use and visitors

can enter if they are properly dres[...]
Leave the mosque and enter an arched shopping arcade. Pass through here and turn right into Ayiou Andreou Street.

5 AYIOU ANDREOU STREET

This is one of the main shopping streets in Limassol with many businesses selling cloth and leather goods. Souvenir shops rub shoulders with local retailers.
After about 200m the road fans out and ahead is a large church, Ayia Evenegelismos.

6 AYIA EVENEGELISMOS

This is a large modern church decorated in typically ornate style.
Continue ahead on Ayiou Andreou Street until a pedestrianised area is reached and then turn right down Iphigenia Street. A shop of the Cyprus handicraft service is on the right, just before the street reaches the seafront. Those who are tired can stop here, those with energy remaining should return and continue along Ayiou Andreou Street. Ayia Trias Church is off a side street to the left and the Folk Art Museum (see page 74) is at the junction with Kapodistria Street. Very soon Tanagrea Ceramics, opposite Androutsou Street, is seen on the right. Proceed a little further before turning right along Tornariti Street to the municipal gardens.

7 MUNICIPAL GARDENS

The Limassol wine festival is held here in the first two weeks of September when there are many stalls and great revelry.

At other times of the year it is a quiet place, well watered and remarkably green compared to the rest of the town. There is a small zoo at the eastern end of the gardens.
Turn down to the seafront passing the Roman Catholic church of St Catherine and return to the starting point.

Paphos

This walk explores the lower town of Paphos which contains some of the most impressive archaeological sites on the island. *Allow 1 hour for the walk; longer if the sights are visited.*

Start at the junction of Apostolou Pavlou Avenue with the seafront, by the La Mirage restaurant. Follow the line of the seafront, leading past the the Pelican Café to the harbour.

Nearby

Ayios Lamprianos Catacomb

Modern lighthouse

Panayia Limeniotissa *(Early Christian Basilica)*

1 CAFÉS

Virtually all the waterfront cafés and restaurants have a pelican motif, although these days the native pelican itself is rarely seen.

At the far end of the harbour turn towards the fort.

2 HARBOUR AND FORT

The harbour is a pleasant place, still used by local fishermen. There were originally two forts guarding the entrance. The oldest one, out on the breakwater, now consists of only two lumps of rock. The other was built by the Lusignans to defend the town against pirate raiders. It is open to the public with the dungeons and battlements as the main points of interest.

Turn inland on to scrubland behind the harbour, keeping the modern lighthouse in view as a landmark. Pass the Kyklos Art

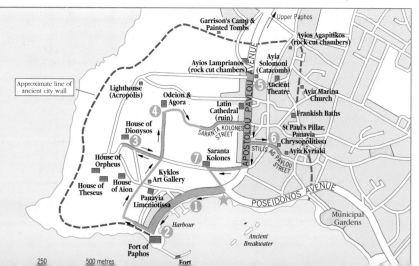

Gallery, housed in an old brown, stone, church-like building, and follow the path round the side until a tarred road is met and the sign 'To the Mosaics' is seen. Follow the sign up the hill.

3 HOUSE OF DIONYSOS MOSAICS

This is a huge complex on the hill with spectacular mosaics displayed in covered sheds. Visitors walk round on raised platforms. The house of Dionysos contains the most extensive range of mosaics, but there are two other houses on the site; those of Aion and Theseus, and both are worth exploring. Excavations are still continuing on the site.

Go back down the hill and turn left on the road to the Odeion and lighthouse.

Fine mosaics, beautifully preserved, are displayed in the House of Dionysos

4 ODEION

Although the site includes the remains of an acropolis, the most distinctive ruin is that of the Roman Odeion Theatre which has been partially restored.

In front of the Odeion was the agora, or marketplace, but only its foundations and a few columns remain.

Take the dirt track back across towards the town. After a 5 minute walk a tarred road is reached, Saranta Kolones Street, with houses on one side. After a further 200m the main road, Apostolou Pavlou Avenue, is

reached. Turn left on to this road and 200m away on the right-hand side is the catacomb of Ayia Solomoni.

5 AYIA SOLOMONI

The catacomb is easily recognisable from the tree outside, which has been bedecked in handkerchiefs. These are put here by visitors who hope that they will be cured of any malaise which afflicts them. The catacomb is still in use as a church and has icons and an altar in one of the underground chambers.

Retrace your steps back down the avenue and after about 400m take the road on the left called Stilis Agiou Pavlou Street. After about 200m the fenced off site of St Paul's Pillar and Church is reached.

6 ST PAUL'S PILLAR

This site, some of which is still being excavated, has the small Catholic Church of Paphos in one corner, where mass is still held. Many columns punctuate the area but it is a small pillar marked by a plaque, only visible through the fence, that most people come to see. This is where St Paul is alleged to have been given 39 lashes on the orders of the Roman governor who objected to him preaching Christianity.

Return to Apostolou Pavlou Avenue and turn left. After 100m take the right turn signed 'To the Ancient Monuments'. On the right is Saranta Kolones.

7 SARANTA KOLONES (FORTY COLUMNS)

This Byzantine fort is an fascinating place to scramble around, with numerous dungeons and arches. There is a large number of the original 40 grey stone columns lying about the site.

Turn downhill across the car park to regain the seafront and the starting point.

Akamas

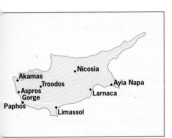

This is a clear-weather route for experienced walkers. *Allow 3 hours. Distance 10.5km. Ascent 400m.*

Start at the Baths of Aphrodite by the distinctive nature trail 'gate' feature. The route proceeds northwest to find an unconvincing-looking path lost in the white hillside. To the left is the exit of a narrow valley. Matters quickly improve as the route moves up and to the right, to follow the right-hand side of the valley.

PLATEAU OF THE MAGPIES

After 10 minutes a flat plateau, dotted with trees, is reached. There is easy walking on the left-hand perimeter and after a further 5 minutes a track leading to the right should be followed. This is the habitat of magpies.

Very soon the path divides and the right fork must be taken. By now the middle of the plateau is being crossed, moving parallel to the sea and in the general direction of a distant and flat-topped hill.

DESERTED FARM

Over to the left, about 400m away, is the first of a group of abandoned buildings. A little later the path swings to the left and heads straight for the main farm. Perhaps once a goat

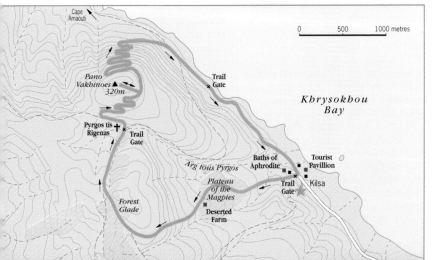

The view from Mount Vakinoes over to Cadearnaouti

farm, it is now a ruin with enormous lizards in its broken walls. Passing through the yard, rocks and a cave can be seen to the right and the path climbs to a cairn marked number 7.

BROWN PATH ON A WHITE HILL

To the left, a valley runs out on to the hill, while in front are twisted dead trees. Brown-stained rocks mark the climb up a hill. As the path moves towards the valley on the left, a choice of route presents itself. Take the right fork and climb up and up. Some confusing options of paths can only be resolved by pressing on through them until the path comes out to run flat along the valley lip. Down below is another path (and water pipe).

WOODED GLADE

Forty minutes from the start of the walk is the reassuring sight of a cool, leafy glade with seats strategically placed. There is a tangle of minor tracks here, but keep a level course, going generally northwest through the trees and eventually join a broad path. Keep straight on, climbing slowly. Soon there will be wooden markers specifying the flora. One will have the number B32. Follow the markers through the pine

trees. When the main track swings to the left it is imperative to take the white stony path in front.

WELCOME VIEW

At the top of the rise the sea comes reassuringly into sight and with a few more steps the welcome view of the flat-topped hill. Now all is easy, the way up the great hill can be clearly seen.

Unfortunately, before the hill can be climbed, there is a 10-minute descent on a good stony path to another forest glade, a crossroads of tracks complete with a stone-built drinking fountain, some seats and the familiar trail 'gate'. At the signpost make sure of taking the Aphrodite direction and see the ruined church across the way. In a while a track comes in from the right but keep straight on up to turn sharply and climb the hill, the shoulder being reached in 15 minutes from the trail 'gate'.

SUMMIT

The path skirts the mountain top before descending. To reach the summit of Vakhinoes, follow the distinctive brown path between the white rocks. A few minutes and the high plateau is conquered with the Akamas far below. It is surely the finest view in the whole of Greek Cyprus, a breathtaking panorama.

DESCENT

The only safe way off the top is to return to the shoulder and follow the descending path along the northeastern face. Continue, even though the path becomes narrow. Height is lost rapidly and 20 minutes will see the walker down to the track and trail 'gate' that runs along the shore from the Baths to Cape Arnaouti. The Baths and car park are about 25 minutes from the 'gate'.

Aspros Gorge

The walk is for clear weather and not for those who prefer a distinct track. Although much of the route is along the lip of the ravine, with common sense it is not dangerous. Nevertheless, no attempt should be made to enter the gorge at any point except the one described.

Location: Western Cyprus, 21km north of Paphos, last 1.5km on a dirt track. Allow 1¾ hours. Distance 5.25km. Ascent 180m.

Start at the south end of the gorge and take the kerbed road towards the water tower. Follow the round white cairns, or walk a little nearer the lip for the best views. After about 10 minutes a walled track is reached by a cairn and this doubles back a little to descend into the gorge.

GORGE BED

This is a detour to see into the gorge. Follow the track down to the bridge and take in the scenery. Return (no short cuts) to the cairn.

THROUGH THE TREES

The route forward from the cairn is not obvious. It turns to the left but is interrupted by a fence. A lower level has to be taken

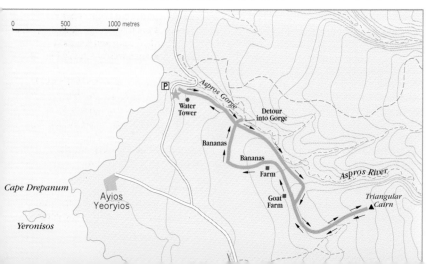

A view of Aspros Gorge: a walk for the adventurous

FINAL CAIRN

Skirt the solid barrier of maquis by moving to the right and the final (as far as the walk is concerned) cairn can be seen directly up the slope under a tree. Note that this cairn is triangular and not circular. It may well have taken 45 to 55 minutes to reach this elevated ground. Sit down, wipe away the perspiration, and enjoy the marvellous view.

DESCENT

Try to follow the path marked with cairns and red paint marks. Almost certainly it will be lost, so take a general bearing on Yeronisos Island and head towards it. Swing south when faced with barriers of bushes. In 15 minutes the cart track above the goat farm will be reached and soon the bells of the goats can be heard again.

Pass to the right of the farm. After some 5 minutes the sound of the bells recedes, and the second farm is reached through fields of crops. Immediately after the building take the track that swings left, currently passing between banana fields. (The paths through the banana plantation could well look different should the crops be varied in future years. If the route is lost keep heading towards the sea and the road from Ayios Yeoryios will eventually be encountered.)

The path again veers to the left and soon there is a fork. However, keep to the right and then straight ahead. After 10 minutes a T-junction is reached. Turn right along a brown cart track that passes through the banana plantation, swinging left to a round cairn.

HOMEWARD BOUND

This cairn is where the detour went into the gorge bed. Keep parallel to the gorge.

to find a cart track (or a path below this may be more preferable). From this point the way ahead is clearer, crossing white terrain and weaving between trees.

BANANAS

In a while a farm can be seen across to the right, with fields of bananas and other crops.

GOAT FARM

Approximately 30 minutes from the start, the path becomes a little indistinct and descends slightly. Behind, the rocks of the Lara headland are plainly visible. Over from the right comes the sound of bells and through the trees a goat farm can be seen.

Soon the path disappears into the maquis and the way ahead is barred. Turn to the right to reach a cairn half way up the slope, leading to another by a farm track. A small goat pen should appear on the right. Pass by and keep straight ahead where a track goes off to the right and then turn steadily back to the gorge until running almost parallel to the sea. Watch the big lizards scatter in panic. Five minutes from the goat pen is a small wired enclosure, but not to worry if it is missed. Continue climbing parallel to the gorge until some low stone walls are encountered.

Troodos

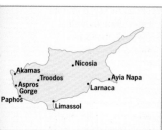

Location: where the road north from Platres meets the main Limassol road. Allow 3 hours. Distance 9.6km. Ascent 400m.

Start at the restaurant and trout farm. Take the broad, concreted track signposted 'Caledonia Falls 3km'. The track zigzags up the wooded hillside and passes a road off to the left. Ignore this and keep straight on as the signpost directs. Very soon a nature trail 'gate' is reached and the road left behind.

FALLS
The famous falls can be clearly heard now and in a few minutes they are reached. It is a cool spot providing relief for the hot and bothered.

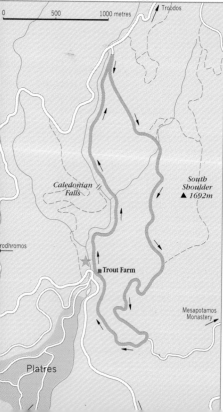

FOREST CLIMB
When ready, return to the wooden steps marked 'Kryos Potamos' and ascend to the top of the falls. The path now stays with the stream, crossing and recrossing the bed as necessary. At regular intervals 'trail' posts advise the name of selected species of flora, although in Latin and Greek.

Twenty minutes after the falls, the stream bed becomes gorge-like and flattens out. Another path comes in from the right but keep on climbing the good path and soon traffic will be heard from the metalled road high up to the left.

SECOND TRAIL 'GATE'
Half an hour on from the falls a green hut will be seen on the right, with a car park up front, near to the upper trail 'gate'. This is an ideal place to rest a while, secure in the knowledge that from now on the route is less demanding.

Turn sharp right, away from the

The Caledonian Falls tumble through the Troodos mountains

immediate civilisation, along the wide forest track and head into the trees. The early ground rises; there are pine cones everywhere and the open views give an indication of splendours to come. Ten minutes from the upper trail 'gate', when the road turns positively to the left, there is a pine-covered suggestion of a route off to the right. This must be taken; a non-too-obvious seat above the narrow path will confirm that this is the right direction.

SPLENDID ISOLATION

In a short while, the route throws off its disguise and there is no doubt that the path exists and is going somewhere. And it is, but in no hurry as it starts its magnificent descent. No motorbikes will be met here, no fellow tourists, glorious solitude is guaranteed. Initially, the path falls steadily and the head of a valley will be reached shortly after leaving the forest road. Now the path turns south into an area where black and white crow-like birds flit silently through the trees. Down below Pano Platres looks deceptively close.

SCREES

Between the pines loose screes cover the slopes but the path navigates them well. Ten minutes from the upper trail 'gate' the path turns left with the bed of a dry stream to the right. Cones are piled up underfoot and the route leaves the bed behind. The track is now a distinctive light-brown colour. In another 10 minutes turn a bend affording spectacular open views.

NEEDLES AND PINES

Care is now required as the way is entirely covered with layers of pine needles, disconcertingly slippery under foot. At these lower altitudes the smell of pine is marvellously overpowering. Half an hour from the second trail 'gate', the path turns to the right, becomes less distinct and then doubles back on itself.

DIMINISHING RETURN

There can be little doubt that this is an exceptional forest descent, perhaps the best in the whole of Cyprus. The route, however, is suddenly broken by a huge tree across the path; the way round it is to the right.

An unmetalled road below is the first indication that the walk's end is imminent. Nevertheless it is still 10 minutes away as the path infuriatingly prefers to run with it and not to it, and in the wrong direction. This is the road from the trout farm to Mesapotamos Monastery. On reaching the road we turn right for the trout farm and the journey's end.

Nicosia

Nicosia is the capital city of Cyprus and has been since the 10th century. It sits on the flat central plain of Mesaoria, with the rugged Kyrenia Hills to the north and the eastern foothills of the Troodos Mountains to the south. East and west, the level plain runs uninterrupted to the sea.

The city, with a population of 170,000, has undergone considerable expansion in recent years, pushing further and further into the surrounding orange groves and eucalyptus trees. In high summer the mid-day heat numbs the brain, the temperatures being several degrees higher than the coast. Fortunately, around 5pm meteorological factors combine to draw in a stiff breeze that slams doors left ajar and brings relief.

At such times, the atmosphere of tranquillity can hide the reality that Nicosia is a troubled place, for it is a divided capital and the Green Line (see page 19) cuts through the very heart of this unique walled town. The battlements were built by the Venetians, those experts of military architecture. They were erected to keep danger outside and safety within. Today a sandbagged line cuts the town cleanly in two and bristles with guns along its length. Sightseers are warned off should they even think of taking a photograph.

Away from the line and its atmosphere of tension and danger, the walled town is a fascinating place. The streets are narrow and the buildings old, some of them crumbling, many being renovated, especially in the Greek sector. The elevations in solid stone hide printing works and carpenters' shops, cobblers and a multitude of other activities. It is easy to get lost in the maze of alleyways.

Interesting squares and palm fringed open spaces regularly punctuate the street pattern and help in the traverse of the town. Movement between the two sectors is only allowed from the Greek section and visitors must return the same day (see page 18).

Those who pass through the checkpoint will perhaps feel they have entered a different country for the language is Turkish and the religion Muslim. The pace of life is unhurried, peasants still walk with baskets of goods and there are old shops that have not changed in generations.

Outside the old walls is the hub of a modern city. In the south, multi-storey buildings and old colonial-style houses stand side by side, with shiny modern buildings going up all around. Makarios III Avenue is a wide street with banks at one end and a Woolworths at the other. In between are smart boutiques selling quality goods. Further out there are hotels, embassies and residential estates. In the north, the Turks have dramatically improved the road system and many new buildings are being constructed, if not quite on the same scale as the Greek part of the town.

History
There is no clear evidence of when the city was founded. However, it was

probably soon after the destruction of Constantia in the east in the 7th century.

The impressive French Gothic buildings of Nicosia are from the dynasty that started with the acquisition of the island by a Frankish knight, Guy de Lusignan in 1192. In 1489 the Venetians gained control of Cyprus, demolishing the existing city walls and building the massive ramparts that we see today. It is a much tighter encirclement than before and was considered impenetrable. However, the reality was different, for in 1570 the Turks broke into the city after a six-week siege and Cyprus was soon entirely in the control of the Ottomans. They ruled unopposed until 1878 when the island came under British administration. Partition of the city dates from 1964.

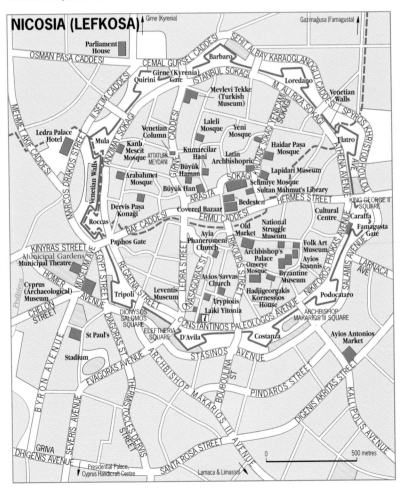

Greek Nicosia

The Archbishop's Palace houses the preserved heart of Makarios III

ARCHANGEL GABRIEL MONASTERY

The church of the monastery, which is set in lovely gardens, is of the Byzantine era but was comprehensively rebuilt in the 17th century and then absorbed into the estate of Kykko Monastery. Inside there is a large fresco of the archangel and, in the narthex, the tomb of the founder, Archbishop Nikephoros.
Location: 6km southwest of Nicosia beside the Pedhaios river. Open: 7 days a week.

ARCHBISHOP'S PALACE

The Archbishop's Palace is a huge mock-Venetian structure which was started in 1956 but only completed many years later. It is not generally open to the public but on special occasions visitors

can see the bedroom of Archbishop Makarios III, where his heart is preserved. In the grounds is an enormous, forbidding black statue of the former archbishop and president of Cyprus.
Location: Kyprianos Square, walled city (tel: 02 474411). Open: office hours. Admission free

AYIOS IOANNIS CHURCH (ST JOHN'S CATHEDRAL)

The first building on this site was a Benedictine abbey where, according to legend, the finger of St John the Baptist was preserved. However, this much-revered item was stolen by Mameluke raiders in 1426.

The current building dates from 1660 and the wall paintings were gradually added over the next century. These paintings have now been restored and

form an impressive collection.
Location: Kyprianos Square, walled city.
Open: normally 7 days a week. Admission free, donations welcome.

BYZANTINE MUSEUM

This is part of the Archbishop's Palace and was set up by the Archbishop Makarios III Foundation. The museum contains examples of icons from the 9th to the 18th century. There is also an art gallery displaying modern paintings.
Location: Archbishopric, Kyprianos Square, walled city (tel: 02 456781). Open: 9.30am–1pm and 2pm–5.30pm, Monday to Friday; 9am–1pm Saturday; October to May 9am–1pm and 2pm–5pm Monday to Friday; 9am–1pm Saturday. Admission charge.

CYPRUS MUSEUM

This archaeological museum has all the best finds from sites across Cyprus.

Room 1 covers the Neolithic period and has a fine collection of Steatite idols. Also of interest in this room is the fragment of wall painting from Kalaasos, in which a headless man can just be made out.

Room 2 moves on to the Bronze Age with a wide range of pottery and jugs. There are some relatively sophisticated depictions of animals and human figures.

Room 3 has finds from the late Bronze Age including more pottery, showing a progression towards more advanced techniques. The middle case contains distinctive and much copied examples of classical Greek pottery.

At the end of **room 4**, after various examples of pottery and sculpture, comes the finest exhibit in the museum: a case full of idols from a sanctuary at Ayia Irini. The figurines are arranged as they were found: a dazzling display of over 2,000 different shapes and sizes.

Rooms 5 and **6** form a sort of sculpture gallery. There is an extensive display of different figures from across a wide historical period.

Room 7 contains sculptures from the Roman period, including a huge naked representation of the Emperor Septimus Severus. In total contrast are some tiny delicate figures in an adjacent case.

Further along are numerous bronze artefacts, knives and helmets. Of particular interest are the stamps and seals which are magnified so that visitors can see the detail. The Egyptian amulets are also worth closer inspection.

To the right and downstairs are several sarcophagi, while upstairs are artefacts from Salamis. Note especially the throne, the ivory chair, sections of a chariot and the huge, bronze cauldron.

Back on the main corridor are paintings, jewellery and more sculpture. The final room has terracotta figurines from early religious sanctuaries.
Location: Museum Avenue (tel: 02 302189). Open: 9am–5pm Monday to Saturday and 9am–1pm Sunday. Admission charge.

Exhibit at Cyprus Museum

FAMAGUSTA GATE

Originally one of the three main gateways through the old city walls, it was built in 1567 by a Venetian military architect, Giulio Savorgnano, who copied the design of a gate in Hania in Crete.

It has now been restored and houses exhibitions and other cultural events in the barrel-vaulted area. To the rear is an open-air theatre.

Location: Ammochostos Street, eastern walls (tel: 02 430877). Open: 10am–1pm and 4pm–7pm, Monday to Friday; 10am–1pm Saturday. Admission free.

FOLK ART MUSEUM

This is housed in the old archbishopric, dating from the late 14th century. The buildings have been extensively restored.

The entrance, housing examples of wooden water wheels and weaving looms, leads into a room containing traditional costumes. There are examples of lace from Lefkara and embroidery from the Karpas. Towards the end of the museum are kitchen utensils and farming tools.

Location: Kyprianos Square, walled city (tel: 02 463205). Open: 8.30am–1pm and 2pm–4pm, Monday to Friday; 8.30am–1pm Saturday. Admission charge.

HADJIGEORGAKIS KORNESSIOS HOUSE

This is the house of Hadjigeorgakis Kornessios, the official interpreter (dragoman) to the Turkish governor between 1779–1809. It is a very fine example of 18th-century Turkish architecture, built around a courtyard with an impressive overhanging balcony. The house now contains the Cyprus Ethnographic Museum.

The museum is upstairs in some very grand rooms. Visitors enter by a reconstructed living room and then tour the house anti-clockwise. In the first room are documents (Hadjigeorgakis' letters and his translations). The second room contains a description of the restoration of the house after it was bequeathed to the state by Hadjigeorgakis' last remaining descendants.

Further rooms contain paintings and sketches; family heirlooms, including sets of spoons; bronze utensils and weapons. Finally there are reconstructions of a dining room and a bedroom, from the 19th century.

Location: Grigoriou Street, walled city. Open: 7.30am–1.30pm, Monday to Saturday. October to May 7.30am–2pm, Monday to Friday; 7.30am–1pm Saturday. Admission charge.

HANDICRAFT CENTRE

This a state-run centre where local craftsmen, some of them refugees from the north, can be seen at work. The work ranges from weaving and woodcarving to pottery. Many items are for sale.

Kykko Monastery in the high Troodos

The pedestrianised Laiki Yitonia

Nearby
Near Famagusta Gate is the Teatra Ena (Theatre One) where plays are performed in Greek.
Ammochostos Street has a small art gallery in a former bakery.
Narrow streets hide enticing local taverns. To the south of Famagusta Gate is a delightful oasis of greenery, while Eleftheria Square has attractive shady palm trees.

Location: At the eastern end of Athalassa Avenue (tel: 02 305024).
Open: 7.30am–2pm, Monday to Friday; 7.30am–1pm Saturday.

KYKKO METOCHI

This is an annexe of the Kykko Monastery which lies in the Troodos Mountains. The dependency contains quite extensive buildings and a church. It was built in the 19th century to administer the monastery's land.
Location: junction of Griva Dhigenis Avenue and Prokopiou Street.

Open: normally 7 days a week.
Admission Free.

LAIKI YITONIA

Laiki Yitonia means 'local neighbourhood' and is a pedestrianised district just inside the old town. It contains several streets of restored houses, restaurants and shops. There are numerous souvenir shops and several good restaurants (see also **Leventis Museum**, page 50). Because of the success of the venture other such areas are planned across the city.
Location: between Eleftheria Square and Trikoupis Street, walled city.

*The recently restored Leventis Museum
houses Nicosian artefacts ranging from as
early as 2300BC to the present day*

LEVENTIS MUSEUM

This is a new museum in a restored
19th-century house. It was built in 1885
as a dowry for the daughter of a rich
merchant but fell into disrepair.
Demolition was imminent when the
Leventis Foundation stepped in to
restore the building and establish this
museum of Nicosia's history.

By Cyprus standards the museum is
very sophisticated; the exhibits are well
laid out with audio-visual aids enhancing
the display.

The exhibits on the first floor cover
3,800 years of history, starting with
artefacts from 2300BC. The displays
from the Lusignan and Venetian periods
are particularly interesting with examples
of noblemen's costumes and early books
which refer to Cyprus.

The ground floor covers the period
from British rule up to the present day.

The early photographs of colonial
Cyprus are very illuminating. There is a
section covering the last 30 years,
including an inevitably partial account of
the fight for independence and of the
1974 troubles.

In the basement are a few more
medieval artefacts and a small café.
*Location: Ippokratos Street, walled city
(tel: 02 451475). Open: 10am–4.30pm,
Tuesday to Sunday. Admission charge.*

MUNICIPAL GARDENS, AVIARY AND THEATRE

The municipal gardens are opposite the
Cyprus Museum and provide a
refreshing alternative to the sights and
museums. Extensive and well tended,
they contain several small ponds and an
aviary with sad looking birds.

Fronting the gardens is the theatre
where frequent performances, both of
Greek drama and international
productions, are staged.
*Location: Museum Avenue
(tel: 02 463028).*

NATIONAL STRUGGLE MUSEUM

The museum displays documents from the 1955 to 1959 period, when there was a terrorist campaign against the British, and from the later 1974 troubles. The exhibits include uniforms, weapons and other implements of war used by the EOKA guerillas.

Location: Kyprianos Square (tel: 02 302465). Open: 7.30am–1.30pm and 3pm–5pm, Monday to Friday; 7.30am–1.30pm Saturday. September to May 7.30am–2pm and 3pm–5pm, Monday to Friday; 7.30am–1pm Saturday. Admission charge.

OMERYE MOSQUE

Like so many mosques in Cyprus, this building started out as a church, St Mary's. In 1571, after the Turkish conquest of the island, the leading general, Mustapha Pasha, decided to turn it into a mosque. It gained its name from the legend that the Muslim prophet Omer stayed here on a visit to Nicosia.

A particularly tall minaret was added in the conversion of the mosque.

Location: Trikoupis Street. The mosque is not generally open to the public.

PAPHOS GATE

This rather dilapidated gateway used to be one of the main entrances into the city. It is overlooked by UN troops and in order to enter the city by this gate visitors walk through the UN buffer zone. This separates the Greeks and Turks all along the Green Line which crosses the city.

PRESIDENTIAL PALACE

The original building on this site was constructed by the British but it was burned down in riots in 1931. A new residence was built and passed over to

Omerye Mosque, named after a muslim prophet

the president on Independence Day. The building was destroyed again in the coup of 1974 but undeterred, the Cypriots restored it once more and it is still used as the presidential office. It is not open to the public.

Location: Megaron Avenue, southwest suburbs of Nicosia, 2.5km from city centre.

VENETIAN WALLS

These are the most imposing structures in the city and are remarkably well preserved, given that they were built in 1567. Initially, the walls took a wider circuit but the Venetians narrowed it to 4.5km. They built 11 bastions and three gates: Kyrenia, Famagusta and Paphos (see pages 48, 51 and 54).

Turkish Nicosia

ARABAHMET MOSQUE

With its high minaret and large dome the Arabahmet Mosque is a most dramatic place of worship. It was probably built at the beginning of the 17th century in memory of the conqueror of Cyprus, Arab Ahmet Pasha. Much restoration work was carried out in 1845.

The courtyard contains a fountain and several tombs, the most significant being that of the Grand Vezier, Kâmil Pasha. The mosque claims to preserve a hair from the Prophet's beard.
Location: Mufti Ziyai Effendi Sokagi. Open: normally 7 days a week.

Arabahmet Mosque is regarded as one of the most beautiful of the Ottoman period

BEDESTEN

The name *Bedesten* means 'covered bazaar' and it reveals what became of this once Orthodox church after the Ottoman occupation of Cyprus.

It was built during the 14th century and was known as the Church of St Nicholas of the English. With the arrival of the Turks it became a grain store and then a market place.

Above the grand north door are six Venetian coats of arms and in the highest part of the gable a delicate tracery can be seen.

The building is, in fact, two churches of different periods, the southern half being the older. The medieval tombstones are thought to be from the Omerye Mosque in Greek Nicosia.
Location: Arasta Sokagi by the Selimiye Mosque. Open: normally 7 days. Admission Free.

BÜYÜK HAMAN

This interesting building is unusual in that its former ground floor is now well below street level, a consequence of the surrounding area being filled and raised. Built in the 14th century as the Church of St George of the Latins, the Turks turned it into the baths which are still used today.
Location: Mousa Orfenbey Sokagi. Open: daily 7.30am–1pm and 4pm–6pm; October to May 8am–1pm and 2pm–6pm. Admission Free.

BÜYÜK HAN

The Han is one of the most impressive monuments built by the Turks on the island. It dates from 1572 and is

*Bukuk Haman, converted from a Christian
church to a Turkish bath*

attributed to Muzaffer Pasha, the first
Ottoman Governor of Cyprus. Its
original purpose was a kind of inn with a
small mosque. In 1893 it became
Nicosia's central prison. There has been
much deterioration over the years and in
1963 it was taken over by the
Department of Antiquities. The
intention is to create a new museum, but
the work has proved long and drawn
out. Although a completion date is
uncertain, it is already open to the
public
Location: Arasta Sokagi.

DERVISH PASHA KONAGI
(ETHNOGRAPHICAL MUSEUM)

Dervish Pasha was the owner and editor
of *Zaman*, the first Turkish newspaper in
Cyprus. It was first published in 1891
and widely read, even in Turkey.

There are two floors, the lower
solidly built in stone with the upper level
in mud bricks. This second floor was the
main residence, the ground floor
accommodating the servants and store
rooms. For a long time the mansion was
neglected. It was taken over by the
Department of Antiquities in 1978 and
restored.

One part of the building has been
arranged as a bedroom, a dining room,
bride's room and weaving room. The
other section is set out as a living room.
There is a courtyard complete with
flower beds and a pomegranate tree.
*Location: Belign Pasa Sokagi
(tel: 020 73569). Open: 9am–1.30pm and
4.30pm–6.30pm, Tuesday to Saturday;
October to May, 8am–1pm and
2.30pm–5pm. Admission charge.*

KUMARCILAR HANI

A Turkish inn built at the end of the 17th century, this has two floors with Gothic arches supporting the upper floor and its roof of domes. There are 52 rooms in total. The upper floor housed the private hotel rooms and the ground floor all the stores and servants' quarters.

Since 1976 the Hani has been the head office of the Department of Antiquities, although visitors are welcome to look around.

Location: Asmalti Sokagi
(tel: 02 72916 or 75043). Open:
7.30am–2pm Monday to Friday; October
to May 8am–1pm and 2pm–5pm.
Admission Free.

The isolated Kyrenia Gate in northern Nicosia

KYRENIA (GIRNE) GATE

When the Venetians built the defensive walls of the city they incorporated three entrances into the circular plan. These eventually became known as the Famagusta, Paphos and Kyrenia (Girne) gates.

Kyrenia Gate is the most northern of the three and it was initially called Porta Del Proveditore after the military architect Proveditore Francesco Barbaro. It was repaired by the Turks in 1821 and a square chamber built over it. The Arabic script on the large panel above the doorway includes verses from the Koran. In 1931 the British cut new entrances into the city on either side of the gate, completely separating it from the walls.

Location: Meeting of Girne Caddesi and Cemal Gursel Caddesi.

LAPIDARY MUSEUM

The building itself is an interesting 15th-century Venetian house. Inside is a display of stone carvings, many from the Selimiye Mosque. Perhaps the most remarkable exhibits are from the tomb of the Dampierre family and the 13th-century tombstone of Adana from Antioch.

In the garden are the capitals from Corinthian columns, winged lions of St Mark and rose windows. The garden wall has an interesting pointed arch with astonishing gargoyles on each side. Various heraldic shields are carved out of the wall itself.

Access to the museum is by courtesy of the custodian of the Library of Sultan Mahmut II, across the way by the Selimiye Mosque.

Location: Zuhtizade Sokagi. Open:
Tuesday to Saturday 9am–1.30pm and
4.40pm–6.30pm, June to September;
8am–1pm and 2.30pm–5pm, October to
May. Admission free.

LATIN ARCHBISHOPRIC

The building dates from the early part of the 14th century, although the upper storey was rebuilt in 1571 by the first Ottoman chief-kadi who lived there. At one time it was the governor's house. The upper storey is ornamented with carved timber shelves. In one of the rooms there is an interesting carved wooden niche, finished in various colours; the ceiling is also worthy of examination. This room would have been the main reception area.

Location: northeast end of the Selimiye Mosque (tel: 02 75895). Open: 7.30am–2pm and 4–6pm; October to May 8am–1pm and 2–5pm. Admission charge.

LIBRARY OF SULTAN MAHMUT II

This is a small building built by the Turkish governor in 1829.

The collection of oriental books includes several richly ornamented Korans and some excellent examples of Turkish and Persian calligraphy. At ceiling level, all around the walls, is a gilded inscription written in honour of the sultan by the Turkish Cypriot poet Muftu Hilmi. If the custodian is not present try the Lapidary Museum across the street.

Location: Zuhtizade Sokagi. Open: 9am–1.30pm and 4.30pm–6.30pm, Tuesday to Saturday; October to May 8am–1pm and 2.30pm–5pm. Admission charge.

MEVLVI TEKKE (TURKISH ETHNOGRAPHIC MUSEUM)

The museum, founded in 1963, is housed in the 17th-century tekke of the Dervish sect of the Mevlevi religious order and in this very building they performed their famous whirling dance.

Exhibit from Mevlevi Tekke, famous for the Whirling Dervishes

A tekke is the Moslem equivalent of a Christian monastery. The sect was, however, suppressed by Kemal Ataturk early in the 20th century.

It is a fascinating place with a musicians' gallery looking down on where the Dervishes whirled. There are many exhibites of musical instruments, costumes, embroidery, glass and metal work.

Adjoining the museum is a long mausoleum with a line of 15 tombs, resting places of Dervishes who had held important posts in the tekke. Out in the yard are several other tombstones.

Location: Girne Caddesi (tel: 020 71283). Open: 9am–1.30pm and 4.30pm–6.30pm, Tuesday to Saturday; October to May 8am–1pm and 2.30pm–5pm. Admission charge.

MUSEUM OF BARBARISM

The exhibits are in the house of Dr Nihat Ilhan, a major who served in the Cyprus Turkish Army contingent. His wife and three children were killed in the intercommunal strife of 1963. Various pictures recall the horrors of these troubled times.

Location: Mehmet Akif Caddesi in the Kumsal area of the new town (tel: 020 71425). Open: 9am–1.30pm and 4.30pm–6.30pm, Tuesday to Saturday; October to May 8am–1pm and 2.30–5pm. Admission free.

SELIMIYE MOSQUE (SANTA SOPHIA)

It may have been an unlikely turn of history that brought the Lusignans to Cyprus but they certainly left an impressive legacy of ecclesiastical buildings. The Selimiye Mosque, known as the Cathedral of Santa Sophia until 1954, is one of the most impressive monuments of Christian architecture in the Near East, and it is little wonder that the Lusignan royalty considered it a fitting place to crown their kings.

Started in 1208, the building was consecrated more than a century later in 1336. Even then work continued for many decades and the towers of the west front were never fully completed. The present unkempt state of the building reflects its troubled past, for it was ransacked by the Genoese in 1373 and by the Mamelukes 50 years later. It was also damaged by earthquakes, the one in 1547 leading to the east end clerestorey being rebuilt by the Venetians.

The work of the original French craftsmen is especially fine in the west front and shown off to effect in the central portal and the great window

Selimiye Mosque, Turkish Nicosia

Nearby

Bedesten, immediately to the south of the mosque: see page 52. Library Sultan Mahmut II, at the east end of the mosque: see page 55. Lapidary Museum, near the east end of the mosque on Zuhtizade Sokagi: see page 54.

The Selimiye Mosque, is an impressive monument to Christian architecture

above. To each side are smaller portals, the detail of which is equally well executed. A series of impressive flying buttresses forms part of the complex nave and aisles structure and these continue to some effect around the semi-circular apse at the east end.

Within the building are massive cylindrical columns with marble capitals. The Turks added three altars facing Mecca and the carpets are arranged diagonally with this orientation in mind. Above the north transept, the gallery is reserved for women. The interior is now whitewashed.

Late in the day light floods in from the west window. At other times ornate chandeliers hanging from on high,

provide light. The two clocks at the west end normally carry Mecca time.
Location: Selimiye Sokagi. Visitors must be properly dressed. Skirts are available for those in shorts. Open: normally 7 days a week.

Muslim Conversion

After the Turks entered Nicosia in 1570 they proceeded to convert the Cathedral of Santa Sophia into a mosque. In accordance with Muslim tradition, every reproduction of the human form had to be removed. All the interior tombstones were either removed or used to pave the floor. A collection of them can be seen today in a small chamber beside the mosque. The tall minarets which are now such a landmark in the old city were added some time later.

The Southeast

*T*his section takes in the lower slopes of the eastern Troodos and the flat lands that reach to the seas of Famagusta Bay. The coastal boundaries of the area run past Petounda Point to the town of Larnaca before sweeping around the bay to Cape Pyla and on to spectacular Cape Greco, turning north to Fig Tree Bay.

Around Larnaca the land is white and arid, a very striking terrain when viewed from the heights of nearby Stavrovouni Monastery. The desert landscape does relent, however, but not until the eastern shores of Larnaca Bay. Here the soil is a rich red and with the good weather and irrigation an early crop of vegetables for export is assured.

Much of the coastline west of Larnaca is an unexciting strip of shingle, and even at Cape Kiti, where holiday development is now established, it is nothing special. Larnaca Bay is fringed with large modern hotels and the beaches have actually been improved as a result. Nevertheless, it is not until the Ayia Napa coast that really good sandy shores are found. Here a beautiful turquoise sea washes over a fine light-coloured sand. It is a very popular area with new, small-town development paying testimony to the industriousness of the Greek Cypriot, for there was nothing there before 1974. Indeed, it is ironic that a little way along the coast, beyond Protaras and plainly visible from Dherinia, is the holiday town of Famagusta, standing completely deserted in contrast to the overflowing resorts to the south. There is no chance of a morning's excursion for the town is cut off by the Green Line. The new city of Famagusta is, in any case, completely closed to all visitors and awaits some political breakthrough to restore it to its original resort status. Meanwhile, the lizards sun themselves on stucco balconies and only cats stalk the dusty streets.

Larnaca is the main town of the area and plays a prominent part in the commercial life of the region. It has expanded considerably in recent years with new development, much of it residential and resulting in a virtual maze of identical streets.

> *The affinity of the landscape is with Asia rather than the other Greek islands. The earth is bleached to whiteness; only a green patch of vines or flock of black and tawny goats relieves its arid solitude... And over the whole scene hangs a peculiar light, a glaze of steel and lilac, which sharpens the contours and perspectives, and makes each vagrant goat, each isolated carob tree, stand out from the white earth as though seen through a stereoscope.*
>
> *The prospect is beautiful in the abstract, but violent and forbidding as the home of man.*
> Robert Byron, *The Road to Oxiana*

During its history, the town has seen many changes, and in 1975 it suddenly acquired an airport which placed it strategically on the tourist route. Restaurants and cafés have sprung up to meet a new demand and moderately successful attempts were made to enhance the once-uninviting beach.

Modern-day tourism may still be something of a novelty to Larnaca but it still remembers a holiday trade of a different kind when it was popular with the staff of foreign consuls. It was, however, not always a healthy place and many young employees of the English Levant Company died here during their tour of duty.

History

The town is built on the ancient site of Kition, an important city of antiquity dating from the 13th century BC, the ruins of which can still be seen. It was a location crippled by earthquakes and consequently it fell into decline a mere 300 years after its foundation. During Roman and Byzantine times Kition was not of significance and with the coming of Lusignan rule, it changed its name to Salinas, relating it to the nearby salt lake. The name Larnaca came into use in the second half of Ottoman rule when the town became again a centre of trading in the Levant and a port of embarkation for pilgrims to the Holy Land.

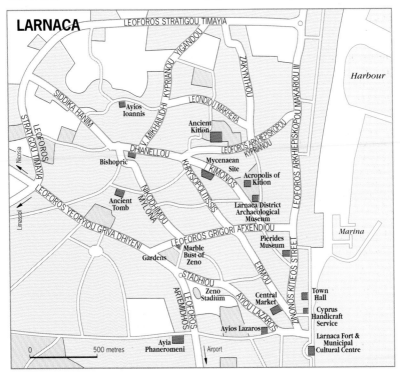

LARNACA

LARNACA

ANCIENT KITION

Most of the ancient city lies buried beneath the modern town. Over the years three areas of interest have been discovered and many of the artefacts from these sites can be seen in the District Museum (see page 62).

The acropolis dates from 13BC. It stood on Bamboula Hill, perhaps with an open-air theatre. In 1879, before it was realised that the area had archaeological importance, the British army bulldozed much of the hill. There is very little to be seen today.

Mycenaean Site

As with the acropolis, not a great deal survives. However, in 1962 and 1963 a treasure of pottery, ornaments, jewellery and alabaster vessels was discovered in tombs by a courtyard. Later, a number of workshops for making copper implements were uncovered.

The fascinating ruins of ancient Kition, the city which was allegedly founded by Noah's grandson Khittim. Excavations continue to this day

KIMON THE ATHENIAN

From Kitium to Kimon the Athenian 449BC–AD1927:
'Though dead, he was victorious.'
So translates the inscription below the marble bust of Kimon, a Greek general.

In 450BC he laid siege to Kition with 200 ships in an attempt to help the Cypriot kings rid themselves of Persian domination. Kition supported the Persian cause, and Kimon was felled in action. As he lay dying, he sounded the retreat and his ships sailed away. The marble bust is prominently located on the seafront along Leoforos Athinon.

Main Site

Now surrounded by housing, this is the
most extensive of the three sites and
visitors will obtain a good view of the
excavations from a raised wooden
gantry. This part of Kition lies by the
ancient city's north wall. The latter was
built out of mud bricks with more
substantial bastions in limestone. They
date from the 13th century BC. One
hundred years later the Mycenaeans
came to this coast and superimposed
massive structures on the earlier walls.
The remains of a large temple can be
seen, which in the 9th century BC the
Phoenicians converted to a temple to
Astarte. Several other temples have been
discovered in recent years. Surprisingly,
little evidence of Hellenistic and Roman
involvement, so prominent in other parts
of Cyprus, is to be found.
*Location: the acropolis site is located half
way along Kimonos Street, with the
Mycenaean site at the north end. Both are
unsupervised. The main site is further north
and approached from Makhera Street.
Open: main site 7.30am–1.30pm, Monday
to Saturday; October to May,
7.30am–2pm, Monday to Friday, and
7.30am–1pm Saturday. Admission charge
for main site.*

AYIOS LAZAROS

This interesting church owes its name
and prominence to events preceding the
present construction. Tradition states
that Lazaros, the brother of Mary, was
resurrected by Jesus at Bethany in
Palestine and promptly expelled by the
Jews and sent to Cyprus. He definitively
died and was buried in a church that
stood on the present site and it was
renamed after him. In 890 his tomb was
discovered and sometime later his body
was stolen only to reappear, first in

Constantinople and then in Marseille. In
the 17th century the church was rebuilt
and the impressive campanile added.

Four domes cover the central nave,
although they are underdrawn and not
visible from below. The main roof is
supported on four massive double piers,
a rococo pulpit being ingeniously
designed into one of them, while another
supports a 17th-century icon depicting
the death of Lazaros. Also of note is the
iconostasis, an 18th-century
woodcarving, and by the south entrance
the doors carry Byzantine and Lusignan
coats of arms. In the south apse the
saint's empty sarcophagus can be seen.
*Location: the junction of Ayiou Lazarou
Street with Phanoromeni Avenue. Open:
normally 7 days a week.*

*Ayios Lazaros with its impressive 17th-
century campanile*

DISTRICT ARCHAEOLOGICAL MUSEUM

The museum houses many relics unearthed from the excavations at Kition. The ceramic artefacts are especially interesting. However, not all the objects are from Kition and there is a fascinating presentation of limestone torsos, heads and terracotta figurines. On the upper floor, a section of the museum illustrates how the Neolithic inhabitants of Khirokitia lived and were buried. Out in the garden one can wander through a mass of incomplete statues.

Location: to the north of the town centre at the junction of Kilkis and Kimonos streets (tel: 04 630169). Open: 7.30am–1.30pm, Monday to Saturday; October to May 7.30am–2pm, Monday to Friday and 7.30am–1pm Saturday. Admission charge.

FORT

The building was erected by the Turks

Larnaca Fort, erected in 1625 by the Turks and used for a time as a British prison

in 1625. It became well known to the visiting warships of Christian countries; they were obliged to fire a salute on anchoring and then await a reply from the cannons of the fort. A certain amount of patience was needed, for this was by order of the governor in Nicosia and had to be obtained by messenger. The cannon posts can still be seen today.

In later times the fort was used by the British as a prison, and the remains of the gallows are to be found near the door. It now houses exhibits from Kition and Hala Sultan Tekke. Occasionally, in summer, the open courtyard is fitted out with seats for folk dancing performances.

Location: on the seafront at the south end of Ankara Street. Open: 7.30am–7.30pm, Monday to Saturday; October to May closes at sunset. Admission charge.

KAMARES (AQUEDUCT)

The name means 'the arches' and the massive arched water course was built by the Turks in 1745 to bring water to Cyprus from wells on the River Trimithius. Altogether there were three sections, giving a total of 75 arches, but today only 33 remain. The tremendous structure, which dominates the outskirts of the town, was in use until 1939.

Location: 3km outside of Larnaca on the road to Limassol.

MUNICIPAL AMPHITHEATRE

This recently built open-air amphitheatre comes into its own during the Larnaca Festival in July when there are concerts and performances of ancient Greek drama. Various events are also held in August.

Location: take the side road off the west side of Leoforos Artemidhos, south of the turning to Limassol, opposite the Cyprus Popular Bank. Open: only for performances (see Entertainment, page 157).

Nearby

There is a little garden outside the Tourist office, dedicated to an EOKA guerilla. It provides a useful place to escape the burning sun and rest the legs.

Location: King Paul Square on the north end of Athens Avenue.

Pierides Museum

PIERIDES MUSEUM

The collection was originally gathered together in 1839 by Demetrius Pierides, a man of Venetian ancestry. Six generations of his family have continued his work and today there are hundreds of objects from various periods of Cyprus's history. The remarkable male nude of the Chalcolithic period is worth a second glance as is the long-necked woman of 325–50BC. There is a display of Roman glass and some examples of early cartographic attempts at mapping Cyprus.

The museum building was the home of Pierides and its distinguished elevations are of the mid-18th century. The property used to be shared with the Swedish Consulate, a link going back to when Pierides was the honorary consul. *Location: 4 Zinonos Kitieos Street*

(tel: 04 622345). Open: 9am–1pm, Monday to Saturday. Admission charge.

ZENO THE STOIC

Larnaca had a most distinguished citizen in Zeno, the founder of the Stoic philosophy, or so it is claimed by the citizens of Larnaca. Zeno was a celebrity and a Phoenician, not a Greek. He was born in Kition in 333BC but left in 313 to study philosophy in Athens. His marble bust near the western end of Afxentiou Avenue is a copy of the only existing statue of Zeno in the museum at Herculaneum in Italy. It was erected in 1921 by the Pierides family in honour of a relative, Mr Zeno Demetrius Pierides.

AYIA NAPA

The town is the centre of the holiday industry in the southeast, although Protaras (see page 70) on the east coast is now running it close. Not so long ago it was a typical small Cypriot village. Now it bustles with apartments and hotels.

The original village centre, by the monastery, is relatively open-plan, but elsewhere there is a crowd of bars, cafés and discotheques that come alive in the evening.

Apart from the monastery, everything is new and the streets are lined with gift shops all selling the same goods; Cypriot traders certainly believe in competition.

Below the town, the small harbour with its sea-food restaurants is constantly busy with boat and fishing trips. The beaches are good and prove a major attraction. Alas the days are gone when the locals could run up and down on motorbikes with hardly a sunburned body to distract them. At the east end, the sea has sculpted some incredible cliff formations, ideal for exploring by canoe or pedalo.

Sunset at Ayia Napa, once a quiet fishing village, now a tourist centre

somewhat plain in appearance. Inside, the ribs of the vaults are painted with the badges of the House of Lusignan and there are some murals, among them *The Last Supper* and *The Passing of Lazarus*. Enquiries for the key should be made in the village.

Location: in Pyrga village, 32km west of Larnaca (tel: 06 234409). Open: daily at reasonable hours.

Hala Sultan Tekke near Larnaca, splendidly set among palm trees

AYIA NAPA MONASTERY

Entry to the monastery is off the village square. It was built by the Venetians in the 16th century, with massive, almost blank, external walls in contrast to the interior. This is a blessing today, for the outside can be a noisy place, but once through the arched doorway into the cloistered courtyard, all is calm. There are some finely carved windows but the centrepiece of the courtyard is an octagonal fountain with four columns carrying a large dome. On each side is a high relief of garlands, coats of arms and animals' heads. To the north of the courtyard there is another unusual fountain, with water gushing out of a stone boar's head.

Part of the church building is underground, cut into the rock and entered by a flight of steps. The entrance portal is of unusual design.

Location: town centre by Seferis Square. Open: normally 7 days a week.

CHAPELLE ROYALE (AYIA EKATERINA)

The church is also well known as Pyrga Church. It was built in 1421 and is an interesting vaulted structure, although

HALA SULTAN TEKKE (TEKKE OF UMM HARAM)

The tekke is splendidly set among the palm trees on the west bank of the salt lake; an oasis in the blistering heat of the salt flats.

It is here that Umm Haram, said to be the maternal aunt of the Prophet Mohammed, is buried. According to Muslim tradition, she was accompanying Arab raiders in AD647 when she fell from her mule and broke her neck. She was buried on the spot and two huge stones were erected by the grave with a third laid across the top.

It is an important place of Muslim pilgrimage, surpassed only by the shrines of Mecca, Medina and al Aksha (Jerusalem). During the Ottoman occupation of Cyprus all Turkish vessels had to lower their flags in homage as they sailed along the coast. Now the sanctuary is enclosed by a dome built in 1760. Green cloth, a symbol of peace, is draped over the great stones.

Outside, a restored minaret stands as tall as the palm trees and overlooks the shady garden with its fountain and water-course.

Location: west bank of Larnaca's salt lake, on road to Kiti. First turning right after the airport, travelling south. Open: daily 7.30am–7.30pm; October to May closed at sunset. Admission free.

KITI TOWER

The tower is not in the village of Kiti. This modest construction is to the southeast about 300m from the sea. It was built by the Venetians as an observation post and has been restored from a crumbling ruin. The bones of Pigmy hippos were found in the floor.
Location: 5km east of Kiti village and can be approached from Meneou or Perivolia. The last 400m has to be on foot.

NISSI BEACH

The Nissi Beach Hotel overlooks the shore, which means a crowded beach at times. Nevertheless, it is a fine stretch of white sands, edged by turquoise seas. The rocky island just off shore can be reached by wading, swimming, or paddling. A few hundred metres to the east, between Sunwing village and Pavlo Napa Hotel, is a little inlet, ideal for bathing, called Sandy Bay. One and a

The exellent Nissi Beach, busy in the high season

half kilometres to the west of Nissi Beach are the equally enticing Golden Sands, a popular place where soaring paragliders look down on the sun beds.
Location: 2.5km west of the harbour of Ayia Napa.

Beautiful 13th-century paintings adorn the walls of Panayia Angeloktisti

Panayia Angeloktisti in Kiti village

PANAYIA ANGELOKTISTI

Although Angeloktisti means 'built by angels', all the evidence suggests that ordinary mortals constructed this church in the 11th century on the ruins of a 5th-century basilica. It was subsequently restored in the 16th century. The building is quite fine and a lantern dome crowns the crossing of the high central nave and transepts. A Latin chapel was added in the 13th century and it is now used as a narthex. Many of the icons as well as the iconastasis (screen) have been repainted and ruined to some extent, the large Archangel Michael at the right of the entrance surviving these assaults better than others. Above the main porch are three coats of arms.

The showpiece of the church is its mosaic, arguably the finest in Cyprus. It is situated in the central apse and can be illuminated for visitors. Angels attend the Virgin as she stands on a jewelled footstool, her left arm holding the Christ Child. To the side are the archangels Gabriel and Michael. Historians cannot agree on the date of this remarkable design, but it is undoubtedly much older than the church and perhaps belongs to the 6th century.

Location: Kiti village, 9.5km southwest of Larnaca, on the road to Mazotos. Open: normally 7 days a week. If locked, ask for the key at the café. Admission free.

PARALIMNI

The village has grown in recent years to accommodate some of the displaced population of Famagusta. It is close enough to the holiday beaches to be influenced by tourism; in fact there is a ribbon of development reaching to the distant shore. Nevertheless, it still pursues some of its market gardening activities.

Bird lovers will be horrified to know that it is here that the migratory warbler, ambeloboulia (blackcap) is caught on lime sticks and served up in the local restaurants.

Recently, a modern open-air amphitheatre was built and this is used to promote cultural events in the area.

Location: 15km north of Ayia Napa.

Beach Life

Sunbathing

This is one of the more popular activities. The technique is not difficult to acquire and the aim is to ensure every vestige of flesh, modesty allowing, receives its full quota of ultra violet. In many climates this can be something of an irksome struggle but in Cyprus the sun shines all day every day. As in many things, modern methods owe a lot to Germans and Swedes. They have perfected the art of lying absolutely motionless between the hours of sunrise and sunset, turning swiftly only at prescribed times. A recent and radical variation is to do it like windsurfers, standing up, breaking occasionally for coffee.

Swimming

The sea is warm from June onwards, usually calm and a beautiful turquoise. Swimmers, splashers and floaters have a great time. The taxing sport of lilo lying is equally popular. Those that have mastered the twin arts of breathing through a small tube and keeping their visor clear, have a splendid time surveying the wonders of the deep.

Pedalos

These unwieldy craft are hugely popular, especially with the youngsters. Speeds of up to half a knot can be attained running with the tide.

The pastime is also an excellent shoulder roaster, so some care is wanted here, perhaps the wearing of a T- shirt.

Sailing Boats and Windsurfers
Both are available on many beaches. Boats are usually taken by those with some experience of 'ready about'. This is not the case with the sailboards. Everybody has a go and quickly discovers a thousand ways to fall in. This can get boring but partial mastery can mean an embarrassing rescue.

Jogging
In Cyprus there are two types; the determined and the zenith. The former practise at sunrise or sunset when the beach is quiet, the latter at high noon when the sun is at its fiercest. The big compensation for the zenith jogger is the periodic header into the sea. This is not simply for pleasure, it is a question of survival, of restoring the body temperature to acceptable levels.

Water Skiing
In the right conditions this is an exhilarating and under- rated pleasure. These conditions are often found at Protaras, early in the day or late afternoon. Experienced skiers will have got used to the situation where the boat is broken down, the boat is coming from the next bay, the mono-ski will be repaired in a minute. This is a sport for the patient.

Parascending
This desperate attempt to escape a crowded beach appeals to a few. At extravagant cost the laws of gravity are suspended for a circuit of the bay. It all seems to work, the only problem being a likely ducking on descent.

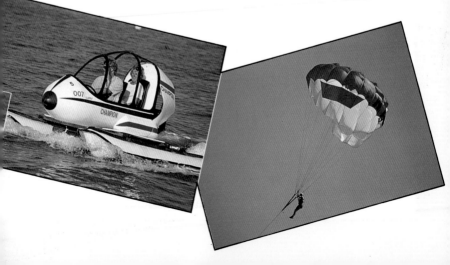

Golden sands and watersports at Protaras

PROTARAS (FIG TREE BAY)

Not long ago Protaras consisted of a beach and one café claiming ownership of the fabled fig tree brought from the east. Now it is a growing town. The beach is ideal for swimming; the sand shelves gently into the clear blue sea. A little way out is a small rocky island. Because the waters generally stay calm the area is attractive to water skiers. The runs down the coast are quite splendid. All the above attractions make it a fairly busy place.

Location: east coast, 14km from Ayia Napa via Cape Greco.

SALT LAKE

This remarkable phenomenon is several kilometres long and about 1.6km wide. In the summer it is completely dried up and a place of great heat, the air shimmering above the white precipitate.

This is the time when the salt is collected. In winter, after as little as one day's rain, the scene is transformed when water covers the salty crust. Pink flamingos, escaping the cold of eastern Europe, make the lake their home for several months. They spend all their time in the middle, so binoculars are a necessity.

Why the lake exists at all is something of a mystery. Geologists explain that the seawater from the adjacent shore passes through the porous rock and is trapped, where it forms a shallow lake below sea-level. There is a similar salt lake on the Akrotiri Peninsula near Limassol.

Location: south of the town. The airport road runs alongside a section of it.

STAVROVOUNI

The monastery can be seen from miles around for it is perched on top of a hill, standing in magnificent isolation 670m above sea-level.

Once through the gate the views over Larnaca and the Troodos Mountains are magnificent. The buildings themselves are unimpressive. Parts are of the 17th century but most sections are more recent, although erected on earlier foundations.

The monastery was built on the orders of St Helena, the mother of Constantine the Great.

In AD327, on her way to Greece from Jerusalem where she had found the True Cross, she landed in Cyprus and donated a fragment of the cross to the foundation of the monastery. *Stavros* is Greek for cross, hence the name Stavrovouni.

It is claimed the fragment is still within the monastery, covered by a silver casing set into another cross, 500 years old, draped in damask. No one can be sure that it is the sacred relic, as the

Arabs destroyed much of the monastery in 1426 and the Turks set fire to the remainder in 1570.

Many of the monks have been here all their lives and produce some of the best honey in Cyprus.

Deep in the monastery's interior resides a macabre collection of skulls. At the lifting of a shutter the sun's rays pick them out with startling clarity. They are those of dead monks, stacked above each other on shelves with their names carved on their foreheads.

Location: 40km west of Larnaca, off the Nicosia/Limassol road. Open: daily from sunrise to sunset, except between 12 noon and 3pm (1pm October to May) and not at all on Green Monday (see page 185) and the day after. Only men may visit.

Scenic splendour beyond the chapel at Stavrouni

Nearby

Potamos, Greek for river, is a lovely little creek where numerous fishing boats tie up. There is a café on the bank where the fishermen relax and exchange stories about their catch.

Location: 5km east of the village of Xylophagou.

The South

*W*ith the exception of the elevated village of Pano Lefkara, only the coastal strip comprises this section. Governor's Beach forms the eastern extremity and Pissouri Beach the western. All along there is a backcloth of hills, 3 to 4km inland. The foothills of the Troodos Mountains start their steady ascent to the highest ridges of the massif. To the east of Limassol the coast is unspectacular, although Governor's Beach is a fine place in a dry white landscape. To the west the scenery is better, starting with the cliff-top site of Kourion and leading on to the beaches of Evdhimou and Pissouri by Cape Aspro (white cape).

To the south of Limassol is the Akrotiri Peninsula where Lady's Mile Beach sweeps around the bay to Cape Gata and its colonies of falcons. This is British Sovereign Base territory, one of two on the island, with a salt lake to rival the one at Larnaca. In summer it turns into an expanse of grey mud flats which give off the distinctive smell of salt. The airstrip by the lake thunders to the sound of Royal Air Force jets which shatter the peace of the nearby Monastery of Ayios Nikolaos. At the northern edge of the peninsula are the Phasouri plantations, extensive citrus groves traversed by straight tree-covered avenues.

The old road west to Paphos (not the motorway) passes through Episkopi Garrison, where the green amphitheatre of the playing fields, with its housing estates on the hills, has a hint of England about it, made complete should a game of cricket be underway.

Limassol, the second largest town in

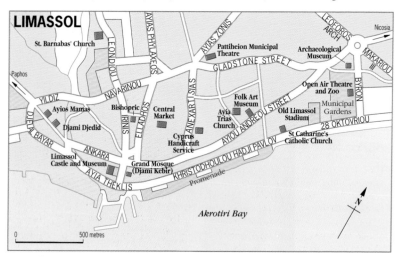

Much sand has been transported to create these beaches at Limassol

Cyprus, is the centre of everything for the area. It is large with a variety of industries and a flourishing commercial life. The port is extensive and busy with ships from all over the world. Limassol is also the centre of Cyprus's wine industry, complete with four big producers. Cyprus's Keo beer is also brewed here.

Known as an entertainment centre, Limassol is also famous for its carnivals and festivals.

The city is not confined to commerce and industry. For many years it welcomed tourists but in recent times there has been a veritable explosion of hotel building – quite astonishing for a place with no real beaches. The famous ruins of Amathus to the east once stood in splendid isolation but today they are joined to Limassol by 10km of hotels along a shore of man-made beaches.

Richard The Lion Heart
It was at Limassol that Richard the Lion Heart landed in 1191. He was on the Third Crusade but came ashore during a storm. There was a disagreement with the island's ruler, Isaac Comnenos, who was subsequently routed in battle. During his unscheduled stop, Richard married his bethrothed, Berengaria, in Limassol Castle, crowning her Queen of England. It seems Lion Heart was unsure what to do with the conquered island; he was short of money and sold it to the Knights Templar. They found it troublesome and gave it back at some financial loss. Eventually the English king passed it on to a certain Norman knight, Guy de Lusignan, and the durable Lusignan dynasty was created.

LIMASSOL

AMATHUS

Amathus was one of the ancient city kingdoms of Cyprus and the remains on this site date back to 1000BC. Amathus prospered because of its port which allowed it to export copper and timber around the Mediterranean. This prosperity was brought to an end by a combination of earthquakes and Arab raids. By 1191, when Richard the Lion Heart landed here, it had been completely abandoned.

The best sites to explore are Acropolis Hill and the agora. On the hill by the remains of a stone jar are the ruins of the Temple of Apollo.

At the foot of the hill, signposted from the road, is a fenced site containing the pillars of the Roman/Byzantine agora. This was destroyed in an earthquake in the 4th century but a good impression of the place can still be gained.

In the grounds of the Amathus Beach Hotel is an underground tomb, part of the western necropolis. There are many other tombs scattered about the site.

Archaeologists are currently concentrating on uncovering the remains of the ancient harbour.
Location: 9.5km east of Limassol city centre, on the old coast road. Open: normally 7 days a week. Admission free.

FOLK ART MUSEUM

This is a collection of Cypriot folk art from the 19th and 20th centuries. Displays include national costumes, tapestry and embroidery.
Location: 253 Ayiou Andreou Street (tel: 05 362 303). Open: 8.30am–1pm Monday to Saturday, and also 4pm–6pm Monday, Wednesday, and Friday; October to May, 8.30am–1pm, Monday to Saturday, and also 3pm–5pm Monday, Wednesday and Friday. Admission charge.

LIMASSOL CASTLE (CYPRUS MEDIEVAL MUSEUM)

The present castle is 600 years old, although it was built on the site of an earlier fort. Its chapel, no longer in existence, was used for the marriage of Richard the Lion Heart and Berengaria, who made an unscheduled stop here on their way to a crusade.

The castle was further fortified by the Turks and now houses an excellent medieval museum. On the ground floor coats of arms, tombstones and wall paintings are displayed in small arched rooms off the main corridor.

Upstairs are some splendid examples of weapons and two complete suits of armour, together with some superb examples of medieval pottery and jewellery, and several stone gargoyles.

The spiral staircase leads up to the battlements from where there are extensive views out across the city.

Downstairs in the basement are photographs of all the Byzantine

Wall detail, Limassol

The zoo gardens at Limassol

churches across the island, with copies of tombstones found in the Santa Sophia Cathedral in Nicosia.
Location: Irene Street, just north of the old harbour (tel: 05 330419). Open: 7.30am–6pm, Monday to Saturday. Admission charge.

LIMASSOL DISTRICT ARCHAEOLOGICAL MUSEUM
Room 1 has axe heads and tools from the Neolithic period. **Room** 2 contains pottery and jewellery, while **room** 3 has particularly impressive statues of the Egyptian god Bes and a headless statue of Zeus, both found at Amathus.
Location: north of the municipal gardens at the junction of Kanningkos and Vryonos streets (tel: 05 330132). Open: 7.30am–6.30pm, Monday to Saturday, and 10.30am–1pm Sunday; October to May 7.30am–5pm, Sundays unchanged. Admission charge.

ZOO AND GARDENS
The gardens are a pleasant, well-watered spot with benches aligned along wide pathways. It provides a welcome relief from the bustle outside. One corner hosts a small zoo.

In September the gardens are the venue for the annual wine festival where stalls are set up by the various wine companies (see page 76).
Location: eastern end of the seafront. Open: all times. Admission free.

Cypriot festivals: typified by their generous abundance of food, drink and merriment

Carnivals

Cyprus's extensive diary of events is undergoing further growth. The cultural calendar has been extended and in addition to the many fiestas there are now athletic competitions, beer festivals, and beauty contests. This is in addition to the national days and political anniversaries. Many of the villages have folk festivals in summer and autumn with displays of music, dance, flowers and embroidery, and agricultural produce.

Traditional events are as popular as ever. Many have religious origins, others derive from pagan festivals.

Apokreo (Carnival)

This is two weeks of fun 50 days before Easter. It starts with meat week, the last chance to partake before Easter, and moves into cheese week where vast amounts are consumed by all. There are children's parades and fancy dress balls in Limassol. With the arrival of King Carnival the celebrations are most spectacular, culminating with the Grand Carnival Parade.

Anthestiria (Flower Festival)

The origins are in ancient Greece where the god Dionysos was honoured. It also marks the rebirth of man and nature.

Today in Cyprus it is held in May and is perhaps a thanksgiving for the memorable spring time when the fields are a multi-coloured carpet of poppies, gladioli, daisies and orchids.

Kataklysmos (Festival of the Flood)

It coincides with the day of Pentecost and is celebrated only in Cyprus. Kataklysmos means flood, and the festival's origins are in the destruction of earth's creatures in the great flood of biblical times. The ceremonies take place in all the seaside towns and last for several days. Purification of the body is symbolised by the pouring of water over one another.

Carlsberg Beer Festival

This is held in the last weekend in June and takes place in the brewery grounds, south of Nicosia. There is music and dancing with food and cold beer at reduced prices.

Limassol Wine Festival

Limassol is the centre of the wine-making industry. During the 12-day annual festival in the Municipal Gardens there is the opportunity to sample the best of Cyprus's wines. Every night, from 6pm to 11pm, the wine is offered free between 28 August and 8 September.

THE SOUTH

AYIOS NIKOLAOS OF THE CATS

This monastery was founded in AD325 and rebuilt in the 14th century. The cat population was introduced to keep down the lizards but now it is the cats which have become the pest. It is closed for siesta between 12 noon and 3pm.
Location: 13km south of Limassol in the British Sovereign Base of Akrotiri. The main gate to the base closes at 4pm.

EVDHIMOU BEACH

This is an excellent and relatively unspoiled beach. It has a long stretch of sand with good swimming from the jetty, although the water gets deep very quickly.
Location: 27km west of Limassol, off the Paphos road.

GOVERNOR'S BEACH

Lying at the bottom of tall white cliffs the startlingly dark-coloured sand can get unbearably hot. The beach, which is not large, can be extremely busy at weekends.
Location: 29km east of Limassol, signed from the main carriageway.

Governor's Beach

KHIROKITIA

Discovered in 1934, this Neolithic site is the second earliest known settlement on the island and dates back to at least 6800BC. Only Kastros, on the Karpas Peninsula, predates it.

It is easy to see why the site was chosen by early settlers. It has a good defensive position on fertile land, with a permanent water supply. The large number of agricultural implements found here suggest that it was a settled farming community, although they also hunted wild animals.

Further evidence of the residents' way of life comes from their graves which were dug in the floor of the houses. In one house as many as 26 burials were found in eight superimposed floors. The bodies were surrounded by gifts. A large stone was placed on the chest of the dead, perhaps to prevent them coming back to haunt the living. The sheer number of graves indicate how densely populated the site must have been.

While the site is extremely significant in archaeological terms, the casual visitor may find it hard to discern the extent of the ruins.

The main points of interest lie on either side of what was once the main street. Five levels of building from different periods have been discovered and it seems that when one house collapsed, another was simply built on top.

In the first area the visitor will see the distinctive beehive-shaped houses for which the site is famous. These were made of stones from the river, with mud bricks laid on top. Some of the houses had several storeys. The most easily discernible dwelling is house A, near the entrance, at almost 9m across.

Excavations at Khirokitia have revealed the remains of a Neolithic settlement

In the second group of ruins there are the remains of pillars which once supported a roof. Some of the most interesting graves were found in this area, including one of a middle-aged woman, buried with her jewellery. In some cases, the thickness of the house walls is up to 3m.

The best view of the site is gained from the far end, at the top of the hill, where the visitor can acquire a perspective of the whole area.
Location: the site is reached 1.5km from junction 14 on the Nicosia–Limassol road. Open: daily 7.30am–7.30pm; October to May, 7.30am–sunset. Admission charge.

KOLOSSI CASTLE

A fort was first built on this site by the Knights Hospitaller and soon became their headquarters. The surrounding area is very fertile and the knights made full use of their land to make the Order the richest on the island.

After attacks by the Genoese and Mamelukes, the castle had to be rebuilt and these are the buildings we see today.

Visitors enter across the drawbridge into a sort of reception hall where a mural of the Crucifixion resides. The rooms all have high vaulted ceilings and those on the upper floors are extremely light and airy with grand fireplaces. In contrast, the rooms in the basement are very dark.

There are some interesting outbuildings in the gardens.
Location: 14km west of Limassol. Open: 7.30am–7.30pm; October to May 7.30am–sunset. Admission charge.

Kolossi Castle; visitors encounter a drawbridge at the entrance

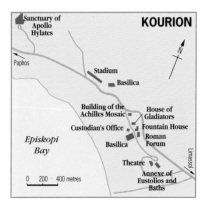

KOURION

- Sanctuary of Apollo Hylates
- Paphos
- Stadium
- Basilica
- Building of the Achilles Mosaic
- House of Gladiators
- Custodian's Office
- Fountain House
- Episkopi Bay
- Basilica
- Roman Forum
- Theatre
- Annexe of Eustolios and Baths
- Limassol
- 0   200   400 metres

KOURION (CURIUM)

After Salamis, this is the most impressive archaeological site on the island. It is wonderfully situated on the cliffs above the Mediterranean.

The site has been inhabited since the Neolithic period, and was colonised in turn by the Mycenaeans, Dorians and Achaeans. By 673BC Kourion had become one of several city states on the island. The main settlement had moved to the present location on the cliff top from the original site near Episkopi village, where some of the oldest tombs have been found. At the same time, the **Sanctuary of Apollo** was built west of the main city (see page 83).

Kourion played a central role in the battle against the Persians. After fighting on the Greek side for much of the war they defected to the Persians at a crucial point, a decision which was paramount in bringing Persian control to the whole island.

The Roman period was one of great prosperity for the city but it was followed by a devastating earthquake in the 4th century. The city was further damaged by Arab raids in the 7th century, leading to the abandonment of the cliff-top site.

Today, however, the ruins provide a compelling glimpse of the past. The first place of interest is the **Building of the Achilles Mosaic**, opposite the guardian's hut. It was clearly a grand building which was probably used to receive important visitors. The mosaic shows Achilles dressed as a woman, but despite his disguise he is recognised by Odysseus. A depiction of Ganymede and the eagle can be seen in a smaller room.

A little further into the site is the **House of the Gladiators**, containing a mosaic of two gladiators fighting. Also visible from here is the **aqueduct** which used to supply the city's water.

On the other side of the track are the remains of the **basilica**, built in the 5th century. It was a very grand building with its roof supported by 12 columns. The bases of some of these can still be made out in places. The whole building was exceptionally large, 70m by 40m. There are still some fragments of mosaic visible.

A column at Kourion, a spectacular cliff-top site important in Roman times

Nearby

Sanctuary of Apollo

(see page 83).

The Kourion amphitheatre is still used for open-air productions

A good 5 to 10-minute walk away is the **theatre**, one of the most photographed sites on the island. What the visitor sees today is not the original auditorium but a reconstruction based on the evidence revealed by excavation.

It seems the original theatre was built in the 2nd century but a hundred years later was extended to allow for displays of combat with animals; the lower row of seats was removed to keep the spectators at a safe distance. The theatre was abandoned in the 4th century.

Today there is a corridor around the back of the amphitheatre, with five gangways leading into the seating area. Up to 3,500 people can be seated here and the theatre is still used for open-air productions. The tourist office have details of the programme.

Just above is the **Annexe of Eustolios**. Visitors walk through on raised gangways. Constructed in about the 5th century it has some very well preserved mosaics.

Steps lead up to the **baths**, where more mosaics are to be found. These include a depiction of a partridge and a bust of Ktisis, a female representation of the Creation. Off the central room were the cold baths, the medium-heated room, and the hot room. Some of the remains of the heating system are also visible.

A short distance away on the inland side of the approach road are the remains of the **stadium**. It was built in the 2nd century AD and remained in use until about AD400. Its U shape and three entrances can still be made out, and a certain amount of its seating. In its day, 7,000 people could be accommodated in its seven tiers of seating.

Location: the main site is 19km from Limassol. The stadium lies unfenced, 800m to the west of the main site. Open: daily 7.30am–7.30pm; October to May 7.30am to sunset. Admission charge. Due to ongoing excavation work visitors may find some of the site closed off.

A lacemaker's house at Lefkara

KOURION MUSEUM

The museum is in the centre of Episkopi village and the collection, started by an American archaeologist in 1937, is kept in a house.

On display are terracotta chariots, lamps, figurines and limestone heads plus a multitude of ancient artefacts from the surrounding area.

Location: at village centre, by the church, 9km west of Limassol. Open: 7.30am–1.30pm, Monday to Saturday; October to May 7.30am–2pm, Monday to Friday, and 7.30am–1pm Saturday. Admission charge.

LADY'S MILE

Lady's Mile Beach is an extremely long and popular stretch of sand. The further away from Limassol, the better the shore and indeed the better the road. The area is not always peaceful, with military jets taking off from the RAF base behind.

Location: Akrotiri Peninsula, 8km southwest of Limassol.

LEFKARA

Lefkara lies high up in the mountains, split into two halves, Pano (upper) Lefkara and Kato (lower) Lefkara. The village has become a very popular tourist destination and features in many organised tours.

Its main claim to fame comes from its lace-making tradition. Lefkara became renowned for lace in the Venetian period – it appears the Venetian nobility used the village as a summer resort and brought their seamstresses with them. The art then caught on with the locals, and they began to produce their own distinctive product, Lefkaritika lace.

Leonardo da Vinci is said to have been so impressed that he ordered a substantial quantity to decorate Milan Cathedral.

It was not until the late 19th century, however, that the village's reputation was firmly established. A forceful businesswoman, Theofyla Antoni, set up a lace-making school and travelled the Mediterranean exporting her product.

These days, equally formidable women try to cajole tourists into their shops.

The upper village is the main tourist centre, with shops all along its length. The streets form a real maze and those driving through the village will need to take care. The best place to park is at the far side of the village.

In the upper village, the church has some impressive 18th-century icons and a silver cross, 500 years older still.

There is a small museum of lace-making and embroidery in a restored house. It is signposted from the main street.

The lower village is much less tourist oriented and its streets even narrower. It is very peaceful, with distinctive blue-painted houses and restful views of the surrounding hills.

Location: 9km off the Limassol–Nicosia road (junction 13). The museum is open from 10am to 4pm, and has an admission charge.

PISSOURI

This is a tempting stretch of sand surrounded by white cliffs and a safe sea, ideal for swimming. The village of narrow streets is on a cliff top, 3km away.

Location: 34km west of Limassol.

SANCTUARY OF APOLLO

This is another important archaeological site. In ancient times it was part of the city of Kourion and was one of the most important destinations of pilgrimage on the island. There is evidence that worship of Apollo started here as early as the 8th century BC, although the existing buildings date from AD100.

Visitors enter on a marked track and will see the remains of the dormitories in front of them. Skirting round to the left is the display hall, the steps of which can still be made out. Ajoining this is the votive pit where the priests put unwanted religious offerings. From here, a short way down the track, is the restored area of the temple itself. The temple was very small and the rituals must presumably have taken place outside.

A roof and fence protect the ruins of the Priest's House, which contains mosaics and pottery. At the end of the circuit are the remains of the *palaestra*, where sporting displays took place. The big stone water jar in the corner was used by the athletes. There are also the remains of some baths, just behind the *palaestra*. As at Kourion, there was a sequence of rooms running from the cold room to the hot room and back again.

Location: the site is 4km west of Kourion. Open: daily 7.30am–7.30pm. October to May 7.30am–sunset. Admission charge.

The Sanctuary of Apollo, an ancient site of pilgrimage and worship

The West

*W*estern Cyprus is a region of high ground, an attractive coastal strip and good beaches. The area starts by the fabled rocks of Petra tou Romiou (Rock of Romios) and includes the town of Paphos, and the whole of the western seaboard. Also included is the majestic semicircle of Khrysokhou Bay to Pomos Point and beyond to Kato Pyrgos. This is literally the end of the line, for the military division that starts in Famagusta in the east, and traverses the island, ends here. The isolated Turkish village of Kokkina, scene of intercommunal fighting in the 1960s, cannot be entered and travellers are obliged to detour right up the mountain before regaining the coast. In the distance, the tiny island of Limnitis with its ruined Neolithic settlement can be seen just off shore.

Fine beaches exist to the east of Pomos Point and they are generally undiscovered. It is here that the western Troodos Mountains run down close to the sea. From the coast road all routes, most of them dirt tracks, lead inland up the valleys and the unwary motorist stands a high chance of getting lost.

The only village of significance in Khrysokhou Bay is Polis and it is growing in popularity. However, it is further west, at once-tiny Lachi that holiday development is now taking hold.

Western Cyprus is a little greener than the rest of the island, catching whatever rain there is, although in summer this is minimal. A striking feature of the area around Paphos is the banana plantations.

Paphos, the major town, is an excellent centre for exploring this part of the island, although each season sees it more busy than before. The airport was built in recent years to generate tourism in what was a somewhat neglected part of Cyprus. It has succeeded greatly, and down by the sea the town has expanded rapidly, some parts nudging against the archaeological wonders of the area.

The old part of the town, Ktima, sits on a plateau away from the sea, a siting that has saved it from being engulfed by new construction. It is a place of government buildings, typical old shops that have changed little over the years, museums and vintage village buses.

The coastal strip below the Ktima Plateau is called Nea or New Paphos. This does not refer to the new hotels, but is an ancient distinction to avoid confusion with Palea Paphos to the east.

For a popular holiday resort the beach is surprisingly poor; perhaps the attraction is the harbour with its medieval fort, cafés and restaurants.

History
Paphos was founded in about 300BC and rapidly became an important administrative and commercial centre. The Romans found it to their liking and constructed many buildings by the sea, However, as with all the ancient cities of Cyprus, Paphos was twice devastated by earthquakes in the 4th century. The town's gradual decline over many centuries was arrested when the British took over in 1878.

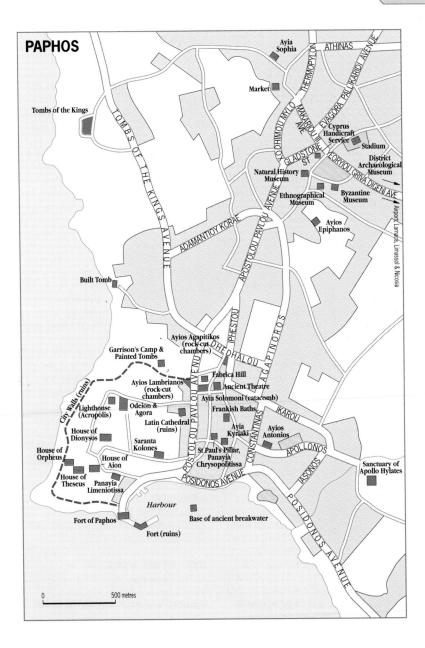

PAPHOS

Ayia Sophia
ATHINAS

THERMOPYLON

Market

EVAGORA PALLIKARIDI AVENUE

Tombs of the Kings

TOMBS OF THE KINGS AVENUE

YODHIMOU MYLO

MAKARIOU AVE.

GLADSTONE ST

Cyprus Handicraft Service

Stadium

District Archaeological Museum

Natural History Museum

YEORYIOU GRIVA DIGENI AVE

Ethnographical Museum

Byzantine Museum

Airport, Larnaca, Limassol & Nicosia

APOSTOLOU PAVLOU AVENUE

ADAMANTIOY KORAE

Ayios Epiphanos

Built Tomb

PHESTOU

Ayios Agapitikos (rock-cut chambers)

DHEDHALOU

AGAPINOROS

Garrison's Camp & Painted Tombs

Fabrica Hill

Ayios Lambrianos (rock-cut chambers)

Ancient Theatre

Ayia Solomoni (catacomb)

City Walls (ruins)

Lighthouse (Acropolis)

Odeion & Agora

Frankish Baths

IKAROU

House of Dionysos

Latin Cathedral (ruins)

Ayia Kyriaki

Ayios Antonios

APOLLONOS

House of Orpheus

Saranta Kolones

St Paul's Pillar, Panayia Chrysopolitissa

CONSTANTINAS

House of Aion

POSTOLOU PAVLOU AVENUE

Sanctuary of Apollo Hylates

House of Theseus

Panayia Limeniotissa

POSIDONOS AVENUE

JASONOS

POSIDONOS AVENUE

Harbour

Fort of Paphos

Base of ancient breakwater

Fort (ruins)

0   500 metres

Buildings near St Paul's Pillar

PAPHOS

AYIA KYRIAKI AND ST PAUL'S PILLAR

The small church of Ayia Kyriaki was built in the 13th century and is still used for Catholic mass. The site is a place of reverence for Christians, containing the pillar at which St Paul was allegedly flogged when he came to the island to convert the governor to Christianity. He failed, and was given 39 lashes for his pains. However, it seems the governor later relented and became a Christian.

The pillar stands at the far end of the site, one of several in an extensive area which is thought to have been the Roman forum. Further excavation is under way.

Location: east of Apostolou Pavlou Avenue. Open: normally 7 days a week. Admission free.

AYIA SOLOMONI AND AYIOS LAMPRIANOS CATACOMBS

These catacombs are very old, but it was not until the Byzantine period that Ayia Solomoni was first used as a Christian church.

Remnants of religious paintings cover the walls, badly damaged by water and by early graffiti. The tree outside is bedecked with pieces of clothing which are left here in the hope that they will cure the afflicted part on which they have been rubbed. Ayios Lamprianos has a similar history but has not been so extensively excavated.

Location: northern end of Apostolou Pavlou Avenue. Open: normally 7 days a week. Admission free.

BYZANTINE CASTLE

The castle is also known as Saranta Kolones (40 columns) after the columns found on the site. Many of these, in grey granite, are still visible.

The castle was probably built in the 7th century to safeguard the town from attack by Arab raiders. After the earthquake of 1222, it was abandoned. It originally contained a square keep with a 3m thick outer wall fronted by a moat. There were towers at each corner, some of which can still be made out.

The castle is fun to explore because there are still spiral staircases to descend and the remnants of dungeons and towers visible. Take care on the unguarded high walls.

Location: Kyriakou Street, on an unfenced site. Admission free.

BYZANTINE MUSEUM

This is a small museum in the upper town. It houses mainly religious items including icons and wood-carvings. Close by are the arches of the bishopric,

surrounding a pleasant courtyard.
Location: 26 Martiou 25th Street, old town (tel: 06 232092). Open: 9am–1pm and 4pm–7pm, Monday to Saturday; October to May, 9am–1pm and 3pm–5.30pm. Admission charge.

DISTRICT ARCHAEOLOGICAL MUSEUM

Room 1 contains steatite idols and a skeleton from Lemba. Room 2 has pottery from the Classical Greek period, jewellery, glassware and lamps, and a collection of coins. Room 3 includes several sarcophagi and clay hot water bottles shaped to fit different parts of the body. Rooms 4 and 5 display numerous statues, jars and pottery from the Roman and medieval periods.

Other interesting statues and column tops occupy the garden.
Location: Yeoryiou Griva Digeni Avenue (tel: 06 240215). Open: 7.30am–1.30pm and 4pm–6pm, Monday to Saturday, and 10am–1pm on Sunday; October to May 7.30am–2pm and 3pm–5pm, Monday to Friday, and 7.30am–1pm and 3pm–5pm Saturday. Admission charge.

ETHNOGRAPHICAL MUSEUM

This is the private collection of George Eliades who enthusiastically amassed a wide range of artefacts from Cyprus's past.

The exhibits include axe heads, amphorae, coins and kitchen utensils. There is also a reconstructed bridal chamber with traditional costumes and furniture. In the garden are two tombs from the 3rd century BC.
Location: 1 Exo Vrysis Street, near the bishopric (tel: 06 232010). Open 9am–1pm and 4pm–7pm, Monday to Saturday; October to May 9am–1pm and 3pm–5pm, Monday to Saturday. Admission charge.

The Byzantine castle overlooking the harbour at Paphos

Café Life

Cafés are everywhere in Cyprus. It seems to be the ambition of every Cypriot to own a café. The proliferation of cafés is mainly due to tourism; nevertheless, the locals have their own favourites, often well off the tourist beat.

Beach Café

These started out as crude sheds, long before tourism, in the middle of beaches. Today they are more substantially built but with no pretensions of architectural design, although it cannot be said that they lack character.

They rely on good weather; half of the tables will be outside with a covering against the hot sun. The service is friendly. Many people partake of a Cypriot beer to wash down the various meat dishes. The proprietor himself is often in evidence and will be delighted to serve a Greek coffee in the traditional miniature cup.

Roadside Café

The construction is generally more basic than its seaside sisters. Notices in Greek abound and in the south the word Kentron, meaning café, will appear more than once embodied on the Coca Cola signs. They are usually frequented by locals, although anybody is welcome. In the country it is unlikely English will be spoken, although generally it is not long before somebody who does pops up.

Food is simple, to be enjoyed with a beer, lemonade, brandy or coffee. Service is prompt and friendly.

Resort Café

The building is likely to be modern, perhaps the ground floor of an apartment block. Tables and plastic chairs, under a bright awning, spill out on to a generous pavement. Toasted sandwiches are a speciality, although more substantial snacks are served, with all the usual drinks.

City Café

This is the top of the range and found in parts of Nicosia and Limassol. The *al fresco* experience takes a back seat. Interiors have seen the hand of a designer. Smartly dressed youngsters in impressive sunglasses congregate in late afternoon to eat delicious-looking, but terribly sweet cakes, while sipping a coke, lemonade, or a coffee. The service is slick, with a professional air befitting a sophisticated city life.

The fort at Paphos harbour

FORT

The fort, on the harbour wall, was built by the Lusignans to defend the town against seaborne attack. However, the Turks still managed to capture Paphos with little difficulty, re-utilising the fort as a prison.

The building has now been restored and visitors enter across a drawbridge and can climb on to the battlements or explore the dungeons.
Location: eastern end of the harbour. Open: 7.30am–1.30pm, Monday to Saturday; October to May, 7.30am–2pm, Monday to Friday, 7.30am–1pm Saturday. Closed Sunday. Admission charge.

MOSAICS OF THE HOUSE OF DIONYSOS, THESEUS AND AION

The mosaics are in three houses: House of Dionysos, House of Theseus and House of Aion, all of which date from about the 3rd century BC.

The **House of Dionysos** is the largest and has the most impressive mosaics. Visitors pass round a covered area on raised wooden gangways. Turning clockwise, the first picture depicts a man, followed by a series of geometric patterns, followed by a picture of a peacock. In the far corner is a mosaic depicting Ganymede and the eagle. The inner set of mosaics show some very animated hunting scenes. Finally, the highlight of the house, a series of scenes relating to Dionysos, including what is claimed to be the first depiction of a hangover in history.

A short distance away, on the other part of the site, is the House of Aion, the smallest house, discovered in 1983. It contains one large mosaic showing five scenes. At the top left is Leda and the swan (Zeus is disguised as the swan). In the top right corner is a picture of baby nymphs with the baby Dionysos. The middle picture shows sea nymphs in a beauty contest, being judged by Aion. In the bottom row Dionysos appears again in a triumphal procession, and the final picture shows Apollo punishing the loser of a musical duel.

Mosaics at the House of Dionysos

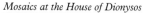

The **House of Theseus** is found in two sheds at the far side of the site. The mosaics here are less well preserved. The best are in the south wing, where Theseus himself can be seen. There is also a depiction of the birth of Achilles.
Location: on the hill, 457m above the harbour. Open: daily 7.30am–7.30pm; October to May 7.30am–sunset. Admission charge.

ODEION

This is a small restored theatre with 12 rows of seats visible. It was built in the 2nd century but badly damaged in an earthquake, being abandoned in the 7th century.

Also on the site, although less easily discernible, are the remains of the acropolis and of the agora. The foundations and stumps of the columns of the latter are still visible and it was probably built at the same time as the theatre.
Location: by the lighthouse on a fenced site. Open: until sunset every day. Admission charge.

THE TOMBS OF THE KINGS

Although no royalty was buried here it seems that the tombs were deemed so majestic that they were given this royal appellation.

There are approximately 100 tombs on the site, which lies on the headland with good views of the coast below. Visitors should take care on the top of the tombs, which date from about the 3rd century BC. These were cut out of the rock and built around a courtyard with Doric columns. They are numbered, the most impressive lying towards the middle of the site. It is possible to climb down the steps and enter most of the tombs, some of which are very spectacular.
Location: take the road signed Coral Bay from Paphos, and after 1.5km take a track to the left. Open: daily 7.30am–7.30pm; October to May 7.30am–sunset. Admission charge.

Make a precarious but fascinating visit to the Tombs of the Kings, cut out of the rock in the 3rd century BC north of Paphos

THE WEST

AKAMAS

The Akamas is a splendid 155sq km area of hills and rocky shores, and a habitat for species of flora and fauna unique to the Mediterranean. It is much in the news in Cyprus with the attempts to keep it unspoilt (see page 102). Only a few dirt tracks penetrate the peninsula, although nature trails are being established for walkers.
Location: northwest Cyprus.

AYIA PARASKEVI

Five tiled domes on ancient stone walls make the church impressively picturesque and as interesting as any of the Byzantine churches of Cyprus. From within it can be seen that three of the domes are over the nave and interact with the two over the aisles, forming a Byzantine cross. A small chapel is built into the thick walls of the southeast corner. The church has undergone various changes over the years and was extended in the 19th century, and again more recently. A clue to when the church was built can be gained from the 9th-century decorations over the altar. Other paintings are of the 10th century and there is a 12th-century *Dormition of the Virgin.* However, the paintings in the aisles are later, mainly of the 15th century and include the double-faced icon of the Virgin Mary.
Location: Yeroskipos village, 5km east of Paphos. Open: normally 7 days a week.

AYIOS NEOPHYTOS

This is an intriguing and much-visited complex in hilly country at the very head of a wooded valley.

The monastery was founded at the beginning of the 13th century by the

A church in a cave at Ayios Neophytos

hermit Ayios Neophytos, a native of Lefkara. He is said to have hewn with his own hands the three caves in the hillside. One was the church, another the sanctuary and the third his own dwelling-place. The walls and ceilings are decorated with paintings, several of which were carried out under his supervision. In his cave there are alcoves and recesses where he kept his pens and papers. It was here that he wrote several books. One title, *Concerning the Misfortunes of Cyprus,* is about the conditions on the island in the 12th century. Another work, *Ritual Ordinance,* reveals his knowledge of early Greek monasticism.

The monastery has grown over the years and the present buildings around the courtyard are of the 15th century. A flight of steps leads up to the church with its three aisles and barrel-vaulted roof. There are 16th-century murals in the apse and some icons of the same period have survived. High in the aisle vaulting are some older murals.

Neophytos' remains are still kept in the church; his bones in a wooden sarcophagus and his skull in a silver receptacle.

Location: 9km north of Paphos. Open: normally 7 days a week.

AYIOS YEORYIOS

To describe Ayios Yeoryios as a tiny place would be an exaggeration. There is a distinctive domed church right on the shore, a café and perhaps a shed, a small beach and harbour. The latter receives small boats carrying holiday-makers from Paphos, possibly on their way to Lara Beach of turtle fame. In the cliffs above the beach are numerous ancient tombs cut out of the solid rock.

A short distance off shore is the barren rock of Yeronisos Island with relics of a Neolithic settlement and Roman buildings.

On the cliff-top, slightly inland, reside the ruins of a 6th-century basilica, together with buildings of the 11th to 14th centuries. Several mosaics can be found close by.

Location: on the coast, 20km north of Paphos.

The harbour at Ayios Yeoryios

Nearby

Fontana Amorosa

(see page 97)

Greek Weddings

Getting married is still the assumed destiny of every Cypriot girl; the dowry system still operates and parents are highly relieved when they get their daughters off their hands. Indeed until recently, girls were chaperoned and casual acquaintance with men was unacceptable. Even today many Cypriot girls lead very sheltered lives.

Most daughters receive a house as a dowry; this is why so many Cypriot houses have an unfinished look about them. An upper storey can be added when required. Fathers with many daughters may have to build an apartment block!

There are two very distinct types of wedding. In town, people are invited through advertisements in the newspaper, which usually means a large crowd. Weddings are held on Sundays and there is a church service conducted in all the ornate splendour of a Greek Orthodox church. The reception is usually held in one of the town's larger hotels. The guests queue up to receive a piece of sweet cake or some sugared almonds and shake hands with the couple.

In the villages the wedding is a more riotous affair. Traditions vary between the villages but often include a ceremonial shaving of the groom and the ritual dance around the mattress of the couple.

The whole village is invited to the wedding which takes place in the street. Long wooden tables are set up and guests are served a substantial meal of *kleftiko:* lamb slow roasted in a traditional oven. The singing and dancing can then go on all night.

*Khrysokhou Bay near the Baths of
Aphrodite*

BATHS OF APHRODITE

These are a trickle of water into a pool
beneath a canopy of trees, a pleasantly
cool place in summer and supposedly
where Aphrodite took a bath before her
marriage. The nearby beach provides
ideal conditions for swimmers and
paddlers. On the cliffs is a tourist
pavilion, overlooking Khrysokhou Bay.
*Location: 8km west of Polis. Open:
normally 7 days a week. Admission free.*

CORAL BAY

There are, in fact, two splendid sandy
bays, separated by crumbling white

cliffs. The sea is calm and inviting, and
sunbeds can be hired if real comfort is
desired. Watersports are becoming the
order of the day and paragliders operate
from a floating platform.

Up on the cliff-top, bulldozers are
likely to be preparing the land for the
next hotel. Many of the houses
overlooking the bay are the homes of
Britons who retired there for a quiet
life, only to find tourism hard on their
heels.

On the headland between the bays is
a Late Bronze Age site called Maa.
Migrants from the Aegean landed here
in the 13th century BC and built a
settlement.
Location: 13km north of Paphos.

FONTANA AMOROSA

This must be one of the remotest attractions on the island. In reality, it is little more than a goat well, and if it must be seen then it can be picked off during a trip to the splendid Akamas (see page 92).

Location: near Cape Arnaouti at the west end of Khrysokhou Bay.

GRIVAS MUSEUM

A distinctive building houses the ship *Ayios Yeoryios* to mark the place near Khlorakas where General Grivas landed in 1954 to start his bloody EOKA campaign against the British. Grivas used the place more than once, for in 1955 the British seized the *Ayios Yeoryios* carrying arms, just out to sea. During this escapade Grivas himself came very close to capture, an outcome which would have spared the island the turmoil that followed. The museum is worth a detour, although the atmosphere of this coast with its strange isolated building is soon to change, for hotels are to be erected all around.

Location: on the beach, 6.5km north of Paphos near Khlorakas, below the domed church. Open: at reasonable hours, normally 7 days a week. Admission free.

LARA

The beaches at Lara are splendid, there being two sandy sections on either side of a bushy headland. The northern one is the most extensive. Here the coast faces due west, towards the open Mediterranean, and the waves tend to be bigger than elsewhere on the island. Wonderful as the scenery is, Lara now has another claim to fame. Green turtles lay their eggs in the golden sands. The authorities are anxious that tourism should not frighten these amphibians away from one of their last Mediterranean habitats and to this end they have created a turtle hatchery at Lara. Turtles are also kept in cages in Paphos harbour for releasing on the western coast. There may just be hope for the poor creatures as access to these shores by land is poor, the track from Ayios Yeoryios being tough going for cars. This, however, is good news for the boatmen of Paphos, for they bring crowds of holiday-makers to the beaches every day.

Location: 27km north of Paphos.

Lara Bay and its turtle hatchery, a refuge for the endangered loggerhead turtle

MARION

This archaeological site features regularly in the official tourist literature and appears on many maps. However, the visitor will be sorely tried in attempting to find these celebrated ruins near Polis. The little that remains are leftovers from the town founded by the Athenians in the 7th century BC. It grew rich on copper until destroyed by the Ptolemies in 312BC. When a new town was built it was called Arsinoe (see Polis)

Location: immediately to the north of Polis. Open: 7 days a week. Admission free.

PALEA PAPHOS

Palea Paphos was the original Paphos. The Paphos we know today on the west coast was founded 1,200 years later. To avoid confusion the names Nea (New) Paphos and Palea (Old) Paphos came into use.

The ruins of Palea Paphos lie on a limestone hillside, near the village of Kouklia, overlooking the sea. It was clearly a large settlement but unfortunately only a very incomplete record of its history has survived the passing years. A solid, well-built Turkish manor house marks the main entrance and is also the museum building.

Its sanctuary was constructed for the worship of Aphrodite who, it was held, had risen from the sea at nearby Petra tou Romiou. It became the most famous of Aphrodite's shrines in antiquity.

However, the building of Nea Paphos to the west signalled the end of Palea Paphos' days of authority. A decline set in, and when the Romans came to Cyprus in 58BC, only the splendour of the sanctuary remained.

To the west of the site are extensive Roman ruins; to the east the city wall runs along the ridge above a necropolis.

Manor House

The main entry to the site is at the manor house, or what used to be known as the Chateau de Covocle, built by the Lusignans in the 13th century. Only the east and south wings survive from the original building; the rest, including the imposing gate tower, are Turkish. The restored building serves as a museum and store rooms for artefacts. From the existing courtyard, steps lead down to the level of a medieval one. Here, a large cross-vaulted hall, 30m long and 7m wide, is lit by several pointed arch windows. This is a fine example of Frankish profane architecture. When the Turks took over Cyprus in the middle of the 16th century, the manor was extended and became the *chiftlik* (farmhouse).

The museum building at the Sanctuary of Aphrodite, Palea Paphos

The Capture of Paphos
When the Persian army attacked Palea Paphos in 498BC they were determined to break through the city walls and a great fight ensued. A ramp was raised and great wooden towers shielding groups of soldiers were moved remorselessly up it to sweep away the defenders. But it was not to be so easy. The Paphians undermined the ramp with four tunnels, then burnt away the props with devastating results. In the end, however, the Persians prevailed and forced the gate.

Sanctuary of Aphrodite
This is the most interesting of the ruins on the site and is found 200m east of the museum. Unlike other temples on the island the goddess was not represented as a human figure but as a conical stone. Next to the sanctuary is the 12th-century **Katholiki Church**, formerly called Panayia Khrysopolitissa, which served the original Byzantine village, built around the ruins of the ancient city.

To the south is the Late Bronze Age **Sanctuary I**, dating from 1200BC. **Roman Sanctuary II** in the north, was built at about the same time but was destroyed in an earthquake and reconstructed in the 1st century AD. Some 400m west of the sanctuary is the **Roman Peristyle House** of the 1st century AD. In the peristyle itself several interesting mosaics of geometric pattern are preserved.

To the northwest is the **House of Leda**, another Roman building. Here the mosaic pavement of the *triclinium* (summer dining room), dating from the

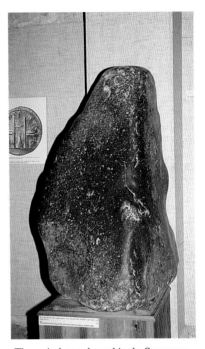

The conical stone housed in the Sanctuary of Aphrodite is an unusual representation of the goddess

late 2nd century, was found. It is almost completely preserved with Leda and the swan depicted on it.

To the northeast of the manor house, and some 600m northeast of Kouklia village (on the way to Arkimandrita), is **Marcello Hill** and the **siege works**, together with the site of the northeast gate. Excavations have revealed elaborate siege and counter-siege works, constructed during a Persian attack in 498BC.

Location: 19km east of Paphos, signposted 'Sanctuary of Aphrodite'. Open: 7.30am–7.30pm; October to May 7.30am to sunset.

Petra Tou Romiou, Aphrodite's Rock

PANAYIA KHRYSELEOUSA (EMBA CHURCH)

The structure is a simple 12th-century design, originally of the cruciform type and complete with a dome. Later additions include a domed narthex. There are many paintings to see, in various states of preservation. The 15th-century decoration of the main dome is visible and is generally in good condition. There is a Venetian shield by the east wall and a carved wooden iconostasis from the 16th century.
Location: in Emba village, 3km north of Paphos. A local shopkeeper holds the key to the church.

PETRA TOU ROMIOU (ROCK OF ROMIOS)

These white rocks in a blue sea are quite spectacular. Folklore recounts that Cyprus's favouite daughter, Aphrodite, was born in the sea foam by the rocks. Today there is still plenty of foam as the water swirls around the shore and runs up the shingly beach. It is a favourite stopping place for many. In late afternoon the view over the rocks from the high ground to the east is

memorable. A few metres inland is a tourist pavilion serving snacks and providing a good view over the rocks.
Location: 24km east of Paphos.

PEYIA

The village presents its best face to visitors approaching from Paphos. Dark poplars stand out dramatically against white houses. Beyond the village a backcloth of hills ascend into the hazy distance. Byzantine origins have been claimed for the village, but no one can be sure of this. To the west of the main square and at a lower level is a public area with an ancient barrel-vaulted chamber, which collects Peyia's famous spring water. Indeed the word *peyia* in Greek Cypriot dialect has the meaning 'source of water'. In recent years the village has seen the development of retirement and holiday homes for Britons. There are several low-priced restaurants providing Greek food as enjoyed by the locals.
Location: 16km north of Paphos.

POLIS

The recent predictions that Polis will become a tourist centre are gradually being fulfilled. The village square has been pedestrianised and the one-way system will certainly trap most visiting motorists. This causes mayhem, but fortunately the locals do not mind a bit. Tomorrow will do here. Barmen have a habit of hiding among the customers, but when discovered can be most generous with the drink.

In addition to tourists from Paphos, Polis has now been discovered by backpackers of various nationalities. Nevertheless, as the village is about a mile from the sea it may be that hotel developers will prefer to concentrate on Lachi, to the west. Polis campsite is due-north of the town close to the beach.

Location: Khrysokhou Bay.

YEROSKIPOS FOLK MUSEUM

Signposts in the centre of the village direct visitors to the museum, an early 19th-century building that once belonged to the British Vice Consul. On display are the work and tools of old-time silk-spinners, saddle-makers and other craftsmen.

Location: 5km east of Paphos (tel: 04 630169). Open: 7.30am–1.30pm, Monday to Saturday; October to May 7.30am–2pm, Monday to Friday, and 7.30am–1pm Saturday. Admission charge.

YEROSKIPOS VILLAGE

The village of 2,650 inhabitants, 5km east of Paphos, gets its name from the words *hieros-kepos*, meaning 'Holy Gardens of Aphrodite'. Although there are some remains of a Roman temple, the village is probably of Byzantine origin. Despite its Folk Museum and famous church (see page 92), Yeroskipos would claim that its most important offering is its *Loukoumi* or Turkish Delight.

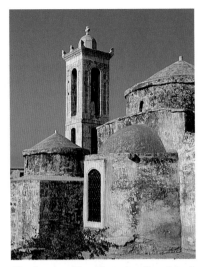

The church at Yeroskipos, the village famed for its Turkish Delight

LOUKOUMI

Yeroskipos is the home of *Loukoumi*, or Turkish Delight. Anything Turkish is out of favour with many Greek Cypriots, so some shops advertise it as Cyprus Delight. The name may have changed, but the product is still a mouth-watering confection of jelly, almonds, sugar and starch, dredged for good measure through icing sugar. It is an absolute must for visitors with a sweet tooth.

A few years ago there were merely two types, pink and white. Today, it comes packaged in little boxes and in a multitude of varieties, including orange and lemon. It can be found in the supermarkets but, of course, the ideal place to buy it is on Yeroskipos' main street, where it is sure to be freshly made.

Sand dune beach near
Kyrenia

Cyprus Moufflon

Akamas Peninsula

Loggerhead turtle:
an endangered species

Conservation

Tourist development in Cyprus has brought great economic benefit, but at a price. The north has so far avoided over-development, but in the south, much of the coastline has changed forever. The west and north coastal areas are some of the last Mediterranean refuges of loggerhead turtles and monk seals. A turtle hatchery has been set up at Lara Bay, and turtles are being reared in Paphos harbour to be released on the western shores. These attempts to protect endangered species are to be applauded, but with the remorseless increase in visitors to this part of Cyprus they may well prove ineffective.

The Friends of the Akamas

This environmental group was the first to start campaigning in Cyprus. The battle-ground became the Akamas Peninsula, which had escaped development because it was geographically remote.

The Friends succeeded in having the Akamas Peninsula declared a National Park in 1989, but there still seems some doubt as to whether the declaration will ever be implemented.

Agro-tourism

This EEC-backed initiative to provide an alternative to mass tourism utilises the traditional houses of the region and encourages visitors to experience the life of the rural community. The emphasis is on walks, wildlife, and the exploration of antiquities in the area. Although these small projects are spreading, they cannot hope to divert attention from the coasts.

The Revival of Old Nicosia

The government is subsidising the reconstruction of houses in the old city, maintaining traditional features and details. The effect can already be seen in the area near Famagusta Gate. It is intended to extend the programme to cover areas outside the walls such as Kaimakli, Pallouriotissa and Ayios Dhometios.

The entire village of Phikardhou has been declared an ancient monument (see page 118).

North Cyprus

Turkish Cyprus has been subjected to so many restrictions that it has not undergone the dramatic changes seen in the south.

Much of the coastline is unspoilt and, up till now, the whole Kirpasa (Karpas) Peninsula remains as it has been for centuries. Long may it remain so!

The Troodos

*T*he Troodos Mountains cover an extensive area, dominating much of the island. If one includes all the land above 300m in the definition then it would account for well over one-third of the land mass. In the northwest the foothills come right down to the sea and a spur runs out into the Akamas Peninsula.

Central Troodos descends rapidly to the central plain to the north, and more gradually to Limassol in the south. The northeastern flanks approach to within 24km of Nicosia.

Prodhromos, the highest village in Cyprus

The highest of the igneous rocks, thrust up by the action of continental plates in prehistory, is known as Mount Olympus, lying at 1,950m above sea-level. This elevated ground extends east for 40km before descending to more modest heights. Despite their impressive stature these are not wild mountains; villages and roads can be found near all but the highest peaks.

In the west and parts of central Troodos the slopes are pine-clad. Golden oak and willow are found in the valleys and where there is insufficient rainfall for trees the maquis colonises the rocky slopes. In June and July the highest ground turns yellow as the dense dwarf shrubs come into flower.

The valleys and folds of the hills conceal a great number of villages,

Prodhromos being the highest at 1,390m above sea-level. Many have a somewhat ramshackle appearance, for they are working places and untouched by the benevolent hand of tourism. Even those on the tourist route up the Solea Valley have the same characteristics as they perch precariously on the hillside. The buildings are quite different to those in the arid flatlands. Roofs have a steep pitch and are covered with red tiles and sometimes corrugated metal sheets. It is for good reason, as the winter is wet with snow on higher ground. There are, however, many clear days when the hills stand out in sharp relief as they never do in the hazy summer. Indeed from the north ski slope of Olympus the view over Guzelyurt Bay and out across the sea to the snow-capped Toros Mountains of Turkey, is a memorable sight.

Troodos is famous for its spring water which is bottled and sold island

Kellaki, a hillside village near Epthagonia

wide. It is also a notable fruit-growing area; the people of the Solea Valley and Marathasa regions specialise in cherries, apples, pears and plums. Grapes are grown everywhere in Cyprus, but nowhere better than the southern slopes of the Troodos. The luxuriant crop is collected in villages such as Omodhos and carried down to Limassol where it is turned into one of the many Cyprus wines.

The mountains are naturally colder than the lowlands, although in high summer the temperatures still reach 30°C and the sun is intense. As a result, the hill resorts are popular with the Cypriots who spend the weekend or longer in places like Kakopetria or Platres.

The potential for hill-walking is being recognised, and the Cyprus tourist office has prepared several trails through the pine woods. However, the heat of summer has to be reckoned with, and away from the trails the impenetrable maquis makes for slow progress.

An important feature of the region is the monasteries and the prolific Byzantine churches that hide in the valleys. These cloistered retreats are splendid places for half-day visits for they contain a wealth of wall paintings, many of them the best and most complete in Cyprus.

A roadside fruit seller

The stone-built Asinou church, famous for its frescos and the pitch and tiled roof

ASINOU CHURCH (PANAYIA PHORVIOTISSA)

This little building, the finest of Cyprus's painted churches, sits on a north-facing hillside, surrounded by trees. The external appearance is perplexing, or perhaps surprising; the walls are solid stone, as to be expected, but the roof has a steep double pitch with a clay tile covering. This feature is merely the traditional weather shield to protect the domes and barrel vaults below. Asinou is an old church dating from 1105, although the dome and narthex were added in 1200.

The frescos inside are remarkable, an impressive record of Byzantine and post-Byzantine art from the building of the church to the 16th century. They all merit inspection. In the centre of the apse is the *Coming of the Apostles*. In the west bay above the door is the *Dormition of the Virgin Mary,* and in the lunette above is painted the *Entry of Christ into Jerusalem.* The south apse has three outstanding paintings; *St George Mounted, St Anastasia,* and the *Mother of God.*

Location: 40km southwest of Nicosia.
Open: normally 7 days a week. The priest with the key is found at Nikitari, the nearest village 5km away, and he will accompany visitors to the church.

AYIOS IOANNIS LAMPADISTIS MONASTERY

Although this is one of the most interesting ecclesiastical monuments in Cyprus it is currently unused. Its origins are Byzantine, the cross-in square church dating from the 11th century. Two other churches are of the 15th century. The rebuilt barrel-vaulted church is the one dedicated to Ayios Lampadistis himself. A tremendous roof of tiles now protects the buildings.

Remarkable Byzantine frescos at Asinon Church

Some early decoration was discovered recently, probably of the 11th century. However, the best paintings are from the 13th century and include the *Triumphal Entry of Christ into Jerusalem.*

The olive and wine presses on the ground floor of the east wing are worth a look, as is the treasury in the west wing

One of the biggest religious fairs in the valley is held in the nearby village of Kalopanayiotis (see page 111) on Ayios Ioannis' (St John's) Day, the 4th October.

Location: Kalopanayiotis, 55km north of Limassol. Open: normally 7 days a week.

AYIOS IRAKLIDHIOS MONASTERY

Although the present buildings date only from 1759, the monastery was founded in Byzantine times. A community of nuns is ensconced here and they find

Working in the garden at Ayios Iraklidhios

Ayios Iraklidhios Monastery, proud of its link with St Paul and St Barnabas

time to nurture the wonderful gardens as well as sell almond honey and other confections. Inside the church the iconostasis contains the icon of John the Baptist which is 150 years older than the church building. Ayios Iraklidhios conducted St Paul and St Varnavas (St Barnabas) to nearby Tamassos during their missionary travels. He was killed by pagans and buried on the site. His skull is kept in a casket in the church.

Location: 19km southwest of Nicosia, a little beyond the village of Politiko. Open: normally 7 days a week.

AYIA MONI

The original monastery was built in the 6th century on the foundations of an ancient pagan temple. However, the buildings seen today were constructed between 1638 and 1820. It is set in an idyllic location, high in the hills surrounded by pine trees and fruit orchards, and although closed to the public it is worth a visit for the magnificient views alone.

Location: 1.5km to the south of Khrysorroyiatissa Monastery.

Greek Orthodoxy and the Monasteries

Christianity first came to Cyprus in AD46 when apostles Paul and Barnabas spread the doctrine with some success. Nevertheless, it was not until the Imperial recognition of Christianity by Constantine the Great in AD313 that the persecuted religion emerged from the catacombs. By the end of the century the Church of Cyprus was fully established with bishops in all the main towns. The kingships of antiquity were replaced by bishoprics and the old temples to pagan gods by basilican churches of Christ, the Virgin Mary and the saints.

During the centuries of Byzantine control, the Church, which had become ecclesiastically independent in its early days, continued to develop.

In 1192 the coming of the Lusignans established the Latin Church on the island, resulting in a long struggle for survival by the Orthodox Church. Its bishoprics were reduced and the remaining prelates banished to remote villages.

Ottoman domination after 1571 resulted in the Latin Church being suppressed and its great cathedrals being turned into mosques. However, the Turks were liberal to the Orthodox Church and the archbishop acquired great power.

The Greek Cypriots are still a religious people, not in any dramatic way, but simply as a natural part of their lives. Many churches are being built, reflecting the new found wealth of the island.

Monastic Life

Monasticism grew out of Contantine's unification of state and church. In Cyprus the life of renunciation was often a solitary existence, although in some areas communities of monks were established as early as the 7th century. Very few of these monasteries have survived, most of the buildings we see today were founded in the 12th and 13th centuries. Even these had humble beginnings. That they grew at all was the result of donations by royalty. They are impressive constructions with tranquil cloisters and courtyards.

In the early days the monks lived terribly frugal lives. This spartan existence had its attractions though and a community could be as many as 400. However, by the end of the 19th century, a monastery as important as Kykko, found its numbers had dwindled to 90. Today, complete with electricity, drainage and other comforts, the monasteries retain only a fraction of this number and it is still falling. Older monks now worry that the modern Cypriot might reject religion in the same simplicity with which he held it. Even so, the monks believe fervently in a revival, and in the interim they carry on with their prayers and the traditional occupations of farming, making jam, and bee-keeping.

Monastical wine products

Kykko Monastery

Iraklidhios Monastery

AYIOS NIKOLAOS TIS STEGIS (ST NICHOLAS OF THE ROOF)

This is an unusual name for a church but one has only to see the huge roof to understand its origins. Nearly all the Troodos churches have pitched roofs but this one is bigger and better than the others. The covering is flat tiles and it protects the lower domed roof. Construction of the original church was in the 11th century, with a narthex and cupola being added in the 12th century. Inside are some fine frescos, many dating from the time the church was built and some as late as the 17th century. The *Nativity* is of the 14th century and the *Transfiguration* much earlier.

Location: 3.2km southwest of the village of Kakopetria. Open: daily 9am–4pm, except Sunday when it opens at 9.30am.

The village of Kakopetria, nestling in the wooded Solea Valley of Mount Olympus suddenly comes into view from the main road

KAKOPETRIA

The village sits at a height of 670m in the wooded Solea Valley, half way up the north slopes of Mount Olympus. From the main road the houses come suddenly into view, picturesque but ramshackle. The village's name means 'bad stone'. According to legend there used to be a stone on the hill above the village which brought good luck. However, one day a newly married couple went to receive the blessing of the stone which then changed its character, rolled over and crushed them.

The buildings in the older part of the village have been restored and preservation orders placed on them. Although a holiday resort, it is mainly a haunt of the locals. Most days the main square, with its political graffiti on the walls, presents a typical Cypriot village scene with crowds of people at the café tables in animated conversation. There are several small hotels and restaurants.

Location: 56km southwest of Nicosia.

KALOPANAYIOTIS

This village is situated high in the northern slopes of the western Troodos. It is a summer resort and best known for its sulphur springs which rise on the eastern side of the valley. There are three springs and the temperature of the water varies with each, an assortment of medical treatments being claimed for the differing degrees of warmth. Apparently 21°C works wonders for general debility and nervous depression. A short distance down the valley is the Kalopanyiotis Dam, an idyllic spot for a picnic. Also near the village is the Ayios Ioannis Lampadistis Monastery (see page 106).
Location: 56km northwest of Limassol.

KHRYSORROYIATISSA MONASTERY

The monastery lies high on the western slopes of the Troodos. It was founded in 1152 by a monk called Ignatius, having been told in a dream by the Virgin Mary to build it on this site. Alternative versions claim that Ignatius found an icon of the Virgin, painted by St Luke and that this prompted him to construct the church.

The monastery then went through turbulent times, suffering at the hands of various attackers. It was totally destroyed in 1770 to punish the monks who had shown political sympathy for an uprising on the Greek mainland. The buildings we see today therefore date from the late 18th century, although due to a fire in 1967 parts were rebuilt much more recently.

The monastery's political fortunes took a further savage turn in 1956 when the abbot was shot in his room by two men dressed as monks. They were acting on a false report that he had betrayed two EOKA members.

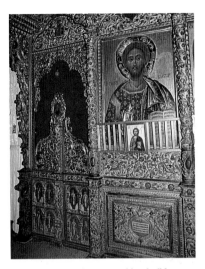

The monk, Ignatius, was told to build Khrysorroyiatissa Monastery in a dream

The demure translation of the monastery's name is 'our lady of the golden pomegranate'. Various rival versions are put forward, however, including 'our lady of the golden nipple'.

The monastery is built around a courtyard with the church in the centre. It contains various relics including the original icon, now covered by silver.

The monks are also expanding the attractions of the monastery, offering the services of an icon painter, and selling books and their own wine in the monastery shop. The Khrysorroyiatissa wine is gaining a worthy reputation across the island and within the monastery is strongly promoted.

There is also a café adjacent to the monastery with extensive views of the surrounding hills.
Location: 34km northeast of Paphos. Closed for siesta 12.30pm–3pm.

The highly celebrated Kykko Monastery

KYKKO MONASTERY

The monastery is the most celebrated in Cyprus and known throughout the Orthodox world. It is surrounded by pine trees in the clear air of 1,160m above sea-level, cool in summer and cold during the winter nights. Kykko was founded in about 1100 by a hermit called Isaiah, in the reign of the Byzantine Emperor Alexios Comnenos. To mark the foundation, and in gratitude for his daughter being cured of sciatica, he presented Isaiah with an icon of the Virgin Mary. This was one of only three painted by St Luke and a very special gift. It has not been seen for centuries and is covered by a silver plate embossed with a reproduction of the Virgin, the original being too sacred for the human eye to gaze upon. It is also believed to have rain-making powers. The faithful consider that the bowed pine trees on the mountain-top have taken up this configuration out of reverence to the icon.

Nearby, visitors will see a bronze arm, withered it seems, and allegedly once the flesh of an infidel who interfered with one of the lamps illuminating the icon. Despite the powers of the icon the monastery has suffered several catastrophes. It was burnt down in 1365 and replaced by a wooden structure that suffered the same fate in 1542. In 1751 it was burnt down again and likewise in 1831. The icon miraculously survived each fiery disaster.

Over the centuries the monastery has enjoyed great authority in the Greek Orthodox world. Pilgrims brought gifts and money, and property was gained in Asia Minor, Greece and even Russia. Today, the monastery depends entirely on revenues from its property in Cyprus.

During the EOKA campaign in the 1950s against the British, the monastery was used by the guerillas for communications and the handling of supplies. Rooms are available for visitors to stay the night and sometimes the weekends are busy. The hill of Throni is close by (see page 119).

Location: 61km northwest of Limassol (tel: 02 942435). Open: normally 7 days a week.

MAKHERAS MONASTERY

The monastery was founded in 1148 by two monks who had come to the island. Later, the Byzantine Emperor Manuel Comnenos, much taken by the place, granted the monastery a large tract of mountainside and an annual donation. Thus encouraged, the small community extended the accommodation and in 1172 it acquired its first abbot. During the plague at the end of the 14th century, James I and his entire court took refuge there. In 1530 much of the complex was destroyed in a fire and suffered the same fate in 1892. When rebuilding was carried out, little from the past was retained. The present design is unusual with large buttresses to the external walls and balconies, and projecting rooms on the top floor.

There are various suggestions for the derivation of the name Makheras, which means 'knife'. One that may surprise hot summer visitors is that it is a reference to an icy cutting wind. The drive through this fine country makes the visit all the more worthwhile.

Location: eastern Troodos, 48km southwest of Nicosia. Open: normally 7 days a week.

The unusually designed Makheras Monastery, twice burnt down, displays large buttrusses and balconies with projecting rooms

Grigori Afxentiou
A short distance from the monastery down a forest track, is the cave where Grigori Afxentiou was trapped during the EOKA uprising. Second in command to Grivas, he was determined not to surrender. The British forces were equally determined to capture him, but after a corporal was shot dead they tried to flush out their man by pouring petrol into the entrance and firing an explosive charge. Afxentiou, although badly burnt, actually died of a bullet through the head, perhaps suicide or an exploding round set off by the heat.

MOUNT OLYMPUS

The mountain is the highest in Cyprus, at 1,952m above sea-level, just high enough to catch the winter snow. This piles up to a great depth but once the sun comes out the ensuing thaw is rapid. The summit is no rocky pinnacle, merely a rounded dome clothed fairly sparingly with pine trees. A road runs to the top to service the radar domes controlled by the British military. Although these blight the scenery, the views are far-reaching and one can see Turkey on a clear day (which is unlikely to be in summer because of the heat haze). The whole area is now a winter playground with several ski lifts (see Sports).

Location: 45km north of Limassol.

PANAYIA ELEOUSA AND PANAYIA THEOTOKOS

Both of these unique and fascinating small churches stand in the Solea Valley, below the village of Galata. Panayia Eleousa was built in 1502 and contains paintings of the Italian Byzantine style. Panayia Theotokos (Church of Archangelos) is close by and even smaller. Both churches are normally locked and enquiries for the keys should be made in Galata.

They are survivors from the Monastery of Podithou that once occupied the site.

Location: 54km southwest of Nicosia, 1.5km below Kakopetria.

PANAYIA TOU ARAKA (LAGOUDHERA CHURCH)

It was built in 1190 and is typical of the mid-Byzantine period, having a vaulted single aisle with three arched recesses in each of the side walls and a dome over the centre. A steep-pitched, tiled roof protects the dome and also a later

enclosure in timber. The marvellous wall paintings inside are some of the best on the island and make up a complete series. From the dome, *Christ Pantocrator*, ruler of the world, looks down; while in the arched north recess the *Presentation of the Virgin Mary* is displayed.

Location: Lagoudhera village in the central Troodos, 48km north of Limassol. The church is kept locked and enquiries for the key should be made in the village.

This humble dwelling in Pano Panayia is the house where Makarios III grew up

PANO PANAYIA (BIRTHPLACE OF MAKARIOS)

This small village, the birthplace of Makarios III, the first president of Cyprus, has become a modern-day centre of pilgrimage.

Relics on show in the Makarios house

The house where the young Michalakis Mouskos grew up is open to the public. It is a humble, two-room abode with his parents' bed in the middle of the first room. There are other relics from his family life, mainly pots, pans and a few pictures.

Just down the road in the main square is the Archbishop Makarios III Historical and Cultural Centre, displaying details of the cultural events of Panayia as well as photos of significant moments in the archbishop's life. There are also items of clothing, scorched in the coup against him.

The domed church of Peristerona

Location: 32km northeast of Paphos. Open: house 10am–1pm and 2pm–6pm, Tuesday to Sunday; historical centre 8.30am–1pm and 2pm–4pm, Tuesday to Sunday.

PERISTERONA CHURCH

Some licence has been taken in including this church in the Troodos section for it is in the centre of the village of Peristerona, on the west bank of the boulder-strewn Peristerona river, the bed of which is dry in summer and a torrent in winter. Its five domes are rivalled in Cyprus only by the church at Yeroskipos. These are set over the nave and one above each of the side aisles. Below the domes, pierced openings separate the two sections. The church dates from the early 10th century but the narthex is a later addition. Of interest is the icon of the *Presentation of Christ in the Temple,* and an old chest embellished with a scene from the Siege of Rhodes. On the west doors are some detailed Byzantine wood carvings.

Location: Peristerona, 27km west of Nicosia. Enquiries for the key should be made in the village.

Wildlife

Cyprus has some interesting wildlife. The much vaunted moufflon has become a symbol of Cyprus and features prominently in the official tourist literature. In reality, it exists only in small numbers in the forests of western Cyprus. It is rarely seen but sometimes heard crashing alarmingly through the trees.

High above the forest, and out as far as the Akamas Peninsula, the griffon vulture is sometimes seen. However, for really good sightings of these astonishing birds with 2.5m wing spans, the Kyrenia Hills are the place. Fabulous formations soar on the updraughts of the rocky crags that run along the north coast. The southern slopes are the home of the venomous blunt-nosed viper. Climbers of the spikey Pentadaktylos Mountain sometimes have unwelcome face-to-face confrontations with the ledge dwelling reptile, which is also found at much lower elevations in the maquis and forests.

Cyprus is visited every year by millions of migrating birds, many on their way to Africa. The eloquent-sounding Eleonora's falcon stays long enough to breed, and can be seen on the cliffs at Cape Gata. However, the most notable and famous of Cyprus's feathered winter visitors is the greater flamingo which takes up residence on the salt lakes of Larnaca and Akrotiri. The salinity of the water is ideal for the brine shrimp which in its turn is an ideal meal for the flamingo.

The best known of the island's endemic birds is the Cyprus warbler, the male of the species being especially accomplished in serenading its mate.

Lara Bay in the west is now famous for its nesting loggerhead turtles (see **Conservation**). Tourism is the biggest threat to their survival, but foxes and crows kill vast numbers of hatchlings. At the opposite end of the island the sandy beaches of the Karpas offer a better refuge to these endangered species.

The visitor cannot help but notice the lizard population, for the sun and high temperatures provide an ideal climate. An impressive specimen is the starred agama which grows to a length of 30cm, living in rocks and stone walls. Even more striking, but not nearly as easy to find, is the common chameleon, renowned for its remarkable colour changes and incredible 360° vision.

Cyprus Warbler

Traffic conscious
pelican

The Reptile House,
Limassol Zoo

The village of Pano Platres

PHIKARDHOU

This whole village has been declared an ancient monument to safeguard the existence of its 18th-century houses. Many have remarkable woodwork features. The restored dwellings of Katsinioros and Achilleas Demetri have parts surviving from the 16th century and received the Europa Nostra award in 1987.

Location: 35km southwest of Nicosia.
Open: restored houses 10am–1pm,
Wednesday to Sunday; October to May
10am–1pm and 3pm–5pm. Admission free.

PLATRES

This well-known village lies partially hidden in a thickly wooded hillside at 1,100m in the Troodos Mountains. It is smarter in appearance than the other hill resorts and has better facilities. The resort became popular as an escape from Micosia's heat and is claimed to be beneficial to those in need of a tonic; perhaps it is the clear mountain air. Because of the contours, the road configuration through the village is a nightmare for drivers in the dark. For pedestrians, access from one level to another is by exceedingly steep pathways. There are several tracks for walkers in the surrounding woods where one can look out over the vineyards to the distant south coast and the Akrotiri Peninsula. The Kaledonian Falls, 3.2km to the north, have a perennial flow of water and make an idyllic picnic spot.

Location: south of Mount Olympus, 34km from Limassol.

STAVROS TOU AYIASMATI

The church is found on the northern slopes of the central Troodos. The church itself forms a simple rectangle but a surrounding protective wall and roof render it barely visible. Unfortunately, visitors have to traverse 4km of unmade road to reach the church, which is kept locked. Enquiries for the key must be made in Platanistasa village. However, the effort is well-rewarded, for this modest building contains one of the finest series of wall paintings in Cyprus. Among them are *The Last Supper, The Washing of the Feet,* and *The Betrayal.*
Location: central Troodos, 5km northwest of Platanistasa village.

TAMASSOS

Tamassos was one of the oldest city kingdoms in Cyprus, dating from about 2500BC. It gained its prosperity from copper exports.

Excavations began in 1874 and three underground tombs were found, possibly belonging to early kings of Tamassos. These days they seem to be inhabited by energetic bats. The tombs were looted a long time ago but the impressive carvings and sculptures on the structures themselves remain.

The site also embraces the remains of a few houses, although they are difficult to identify. Ayios Iraklidhios Monastery is close by (see page 107).
Location: 19km southwest of Nicosia. Open: 9am–12 noon and 4pm–7pm, Tuesday to Sunday; October to May 9am–1pm and 2pm–4.30pm. Admission charge.

THRONI

This is the name of a hill overlooking Kykko Monastery (see page 112). At the very top is a famous icon in a small chapel. President Makarios III was born in the foothills of the western Troodos and asked to be buried close to the icon, overlooking his favourite hills and village of birth. He died unexpectedly with his resting place unfinished. Bulldozers worked around the clock, completing it just before the cortege arrived from Nicosia in a torrential downpour. Today, two soldiers stand, ostensibly at attention, outside his tomb night and day. It is indeed a spectacular burial place; from this vantage point the whole of western Cyprus can be seen.
Location: 1.5km from Kykko Monastery in the western Troodos.

The burial place of Makarios III is adjacent to this famous icon on Throni Hill

TROODHITISSA MONASTERY

This collection of uninspired buildings is found high in the western Troodos. It was established in the 13th century but the present church dates from 1731. Inside is a famous icon of the Virgin Mary, brought from Asia Minor and plated with silver, together with the Holy Belt.

A large religious fair is held in the grounds on 15 August.
Location: western Troodos, between Platres and Prodhromos. Open: normally 7 days a week.

North Cyprus

*T*his section covers all the territory north of the military line dividing the island. It is an area under the control of the Turkish Cypriots, and Greek Cypriot publications on the subject are at pains to point out that it comprises 40 per cent of the island with only 17 per cent of the population.

An obvious conclusion that can be safely drawn from this is that north Cyprus must be less populated than the south. When this truth is added to the fact that there are many less tourists then it becomes clear that the north should be a land of open spaces and quiet beaches.

And it is; and nowhere is this more evident than at the ancient sites. Those of Soli and Vouni rival those in the Greek part of the island, and Salamis is even more impressive. However, they receive distinctly fewer visitors, and though they are controlled in a fashion, the visitor can still walk on a priceless 2,000-year-old mosaic without hindrance. It may well be, of course, that the enthusiast will appreciate this freedom from crowds and officialdom. The sites are somewhat overgrown, but seemingly no worse for this.

Notwithstanding the paucity of tourists, Kyrenia (Girne) on the north coast is relatively busy. Famagusta, in the east, which should be busier still, is not at all, for nobody is allowed into Varosha, the tourist quarter. The splendid beach, once crowded with swimmers and sunbathers, is now empty and has been since 1974.

Some would say that the Turks have the best of the island's scenery. This is debatable, but certainly the Kyrenia Hills are an impressive sight, extraordinary in that they traverse 90km of the northern littoral, yet nowhere are they more than 3km wide; a rocky backbone stretching from Lapta to Kantara and reaching heights of 1,000m above sea-level. The rock is limestone and marble, the northern slopes covered with cypress trees and aleppo pine.

The north coast is not a place of beaches and the few good ones are seldom easy to find. However, there is an abundance of sand in Guzelyurt Bay in the west and an equally good beach by Salamis in the east.

The central plain, or Mesaoria, is contained entirely in the Turkish section. A midday drive through this summer wilderness is a hot affair of mirages and minor dusty whirlwinds. In all this desolation the population figure of 17 per cent begins to look like an

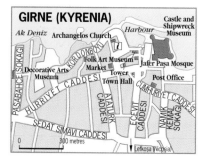

GIRNE (KYRENIA)

Ak Deniz   Archangelos Church   *Harbour*   Castle and Shipwreck Museum

Decorative Arts Museum   Folk Art Museum   Market   Tower   Jafer Pasa Mosque

Town Hall   Post Office

PASABAHCE SOKAGI   KORDONBOYU   HURRIYET CADDESI   ATATURK CADDESI   ECEVIT CADDESI   NAMIK KEMAL SOKAGI   CUMHURIYET CADDESI

SEDAT SIMAVI CADDESI

0   300 metres

Lefkosa (Nicosia)

Shopping made easy in Turkish Nicosia

overestimate. Few would believe that in springtime the land is transformed into a blaze of colour with wild mustard, poppies, chrysanthemums and a hundred other species bursting forth.

All the Greek placenames have been changed by the authorities. For example, Lapithos, a favourite haunt of Lawrence Durrell, is now Lapta, and Akanthou is Tatlisu. Maps that embrace these changes are rare even after all these years. Nevertheless, should the traveller inadvertently stray off the beaten track he will receive a cheerful and noisy welcome from the local children and an equally animated farewell.

The Karpas (Kirpasa), or 'panhandle' as it is known, is another unique geographical feature. It reaches out towards Syria for nearly 80km, yet is only a fraction of this in width, the blue sea on both shores being visible from high ground. Along the shore small beaches remain to be discovered together with several intriguing sites of antiquity. The area was once well populated and forested, with ships calling to collect cedar wood. Gradually its importance declined, perhaps with a change of climate, and for centuries it has been remote and isolated. Events have passed it by so much so that a small Greek Cypriot community still lives there, having refused to flee in the 1974 turmoil. There is only one other such community in the north, despite being Maronites. Their villages are at the very opposite end of the north coast, near Cape Kormakiti.

Troops from Turkey still occupy part of the north and although efforts have been made to accommodate the tourist some places of interest are still out of bounds.

FAMAGUSTA (GAZIMAGUSA)

Please note that it is difficult to see the interior of the churches, admission not being readily available, and some of the buildings are close to the military areas, making any access difficult.

AYIA ZONI AND AYIOS NIKOLAOS

Ayia Zoni is a small church built in the 15th century, dedicated to the Blessed Virgin Mary. It is designed in the form of a cross with a central dome and barrel-vaulted roof. During the famous siege of the town it escaped damage, remaining in fairly reasonable order. Inside are the remnants of wall paintings.

Nearby, Ayios Nikolaos is of the 14th century. Part of the nave and the semicircular apse have survived.
Location: Hisar Yolou Sokagi.

BIDDULPH'S GATE

This was named after Sir Robert Biddulph, British High Commissioner in Cyprus in 1879, who saved the monument from destruction. It is an imitation of a Roman triumphal arch and probably marked the entrance to a merchant's house. Two large marble columns once formed part of the gateway but they have now gone, the monument being much vandalised over the years.
Location: Naim Efendi Sokagi.

CARMELITE CHURCH (ST MARY'S)

This was one of the most important churches in Famagusta. A monastery once stood on the site but of this nothing remains. The ruined church dates from the mid-14th century, built soon after

the short Genoese occupation.
Location: Server Somoundjouoglou. Access is difficult because of the military.

DJAFER PAŞA BATHS

The building was put into service in 1601 by Djafer Paşa for the people of Famagusta. It is in somewhat better state of preservation than the other old baths of the town.
Location: Naim Efendi Sokagi, opposite Lala Mustafa Paşa Mosque.

DJAFER PAŞA FOUNTAIN

Djafer Paşa was a Turkish administrator who ordered the construction of water arches to supply the town with water. The original arches were destroyed, however, along with the fountain itself. A replacement fountain was built some time later using the surviving fountain-head which bears the date 1597 and the name of Djafer Paşa.
Location: Naim Efendi Sokagi, opposite Lala Mustafa Paşa Mosque.

DJAMBOULAT MUSEUM

Fine examples of Turkish folk art, including embroidery and clothing.
Location: Djamboulat bastion in the walls (tel: 036 65498). Open: 7.30am–2pm, Monday to Friday; October to May 8am–1pm and 2pm–5pm. Admission charge.

LALA MUSTAFA PAŞA MOSQUE (ST NICHOLAS' CATHEDRAL)

It is remarkable that the Lusignans, so far from home, should have erected this large and formidable building. Construction work was started some time towards the end of the 13th century and may well have taken 100 years to complete. The Lusignans must have been well satisfied with their achievement, for the cathedral they called St Nicholas is a fine example of French Gothic architecture. Their kings, already crowned in Nicosia, indulged themselves by being crowned 'kings of Jerusalem' here.

The cathedral was much damaged in the siege of 1570 and soon after the conquest the Turks converted it into a mosque, adding the minaret that we see today. Over the years it has suffered; the two great towers of the west front, once compared with those of Rheims, lost part of their tops during the siege. Despite everything, the west front is still a magnificent elevation with its three porches and marvellous central six-light window carrying a rose trellis above. To each side are tall walled-in windows surmounted by the windows of the damaged towers.

In the conversion to a mosque all images of the human form, whether in stone, fresco or stained glass, were removed. It is likely that the porch niches housed statues of saints, and doubtless they were taken away at this time.

Today the interior is decorated simply and the floor covered with carpets. A few medieval tombs in the north aisle survived the conversion. *Location: Naim Efendi Sokagi. Open: normally 7 days a week. Admission free.*

MEDRESE
This building was originally a Muslim high school for theological study. It was built by the Ottomans on the remains of a building from the Lusignan period. Today it is used as offices. *Location: Liman Yolu Sokagi. Open: 7.30am–2pm, Monday to Friday; October to May 8am–1pm and 2pm–5pm. Admission free.*

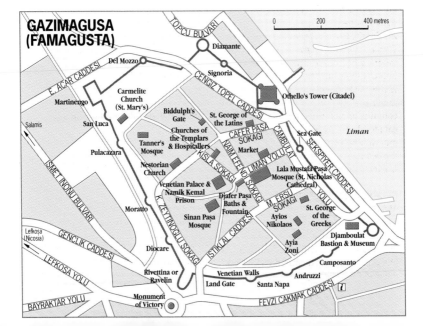

A climb to the top of Othello's Tower gives spectacular views of Famagusta

NESTORIAN CHURCH (ST GEORGE'S)

The Nestorians, or Chaldeans, came from Syria and the church was built for them in 1350 by a rich businessman called Francis Lakkas. Another name for the church is Ayios Yeoryios Xorinos, meaning St George the Exiler. It is claimed that dust from the floor of the church has the power to bring down one's enemies.

Location: off Somoundjouoglou Sokagi by the Moratto Bastion.

OTHELLO'S TOWER

This distinctive construction in the city walls carries the winged lion of St Mark carved in stone above the entrance, the badge of Venice. Inside is the Great Hall, perhaps a refectory, the vaulted roof supported by Gothic arches. Steps lead to the battlements and there are dramatic views over the city and the harbour. In earlier days the harbour entrance was safe-guarded by a huge chain hung from towers.

Shakespeare's tragedy was set in Cyprus and there is a suggestion that the military governor of the island, Christopher Moro, was the fateful Moor in the play. The link is fairly tenuous; Shakespeare had never been to Cyprus and would have known little about it.

Location: in the ancient city walls, halfway along the east side on Cengiz Topel Caddesi. Open: 9am–1.30pm and 4.30pm–6.30pm; October to May 8am–1pm and 2.30pm–5pm. Admission charge.

SINAN PAŞA MOSQUE (THE CHURCH OF ST PETER AND ST PAUL)

This building started life as a Latin church in the reign of Peter I and is an adventurous structure of flying buttresses. With the arrival of the Turks in 1571 it was converted into a mosque; the remains of the minaret can be found in one corner. During British rule it was used as a grain and potato store, and became known as the 'wheat mosque'. Some restoration work was carried out in 1961 and for a while the building was the city hall. Today it is the municipal library.

In the yard is the tomb of Mehmet Efendi, a famous literary diplomat of the 18th century. He died in 1732.

Location: Abdullah Paşa Sokagi. Open: 7.30am–2pm, Monday to Friday; October to May 8am–1pm and 2pm–5pm.

ST GEORGE OF THE GREEKS

The large Church of St George may have been built in opposition to the

The ruins of St George of the Greeks, once Famagusta's Orthodox cathedral

Latin Cathedral of St Nicholas, for it was once the Orthodox cathedral. It is a dramatic ruin of conflicting styles. Most of it is Gothic but the decorated apses are of the Byzantine style. The side of the church that faced the Djamboulat Bastion took a terrific hammering in the siege of 1570 and it was probably at this time that the dome was destroyed.
Location: Mustafa Ersu Sokagi.

ST GEORGE OF THE LATINS
Little is known of the history of this church. The ruins suggest that it must have been a splendid place. The lancet windows are tall and their sills set unusually high, perhaps for defensive purposes. It may have been built at the end of the 13th century and it certainly suffered damage during the siege of the town in 1570.

Location: Kapou Sokagi, near Othello's Tower.

TANNER'S MOSQUE
Originally a 16th-century church, the building was converted when the Turks occupied Cyprus. As with other churches of this period, vases and earthenware bottles were used in the infill to the roof-vaulting, possibly for acoustic reasons.
Location: Somoundjouoglou Sokagi. Access is difficult because of the military.

TWIN CHURCHES OF THE TEMPLARS AND HOSPITALLERS
These two small 14th-century churches have been restored in recent times. They were built after the expulsion of the Templars and Hospitallers from Palestine.
Location: Kisla Sokagi.

VENETIAN PALACE AND NAMIK KEMAL PRISON (PALAZZO DEL PROVEDITORE)
Dating from the 13th century, the building was originally the royal palace of the Lusignans. Earthquakes destroyed the main structure leaving only the western portion standing, although this is impressive enough. Three arches can be seen carried on columns that may well have come from Salamis. Over the central arch the keystone bears the coat of arms of Giovanni Renier, a Captain of Cyprus in 1552. It was here that Namik Kemal, a Turkish author and poet, was imprisoned after being deported from Istanbul in 1873. This part of the building now functions as a museum.
Location: Sinan Pasa Sokagi. Open: 7.30am–2pm, Monday to Friday; October to May 8am–1pm and 2pm–5pm. Admission free.

VENETIAN WALLS

Fifteen bastions are built into the 15m high ramparts, which in some places are 8m thick. There are five entrances with the main Land Gate at the southwest corner of the rectangular enclosure. This gate lies adjacent to the original arched gateway and access to it is over a 19th-century bridge. Behind the gateway is the Ravelin, or Rivettina Bastion, housing a collection of guardrooms and dungeons. It was here in 1571 that the Turks first breached the walls and the surrender flag was hoisted. Within the gate there is a maze of passages connecting the gun chambers.

A ramp through the arch leads to the top of the Ravelin, opening on to a walk along the ramparts. Five more bastions are located along the southwest wall; the Diocare, Moratto, Pulacazara and San Luca bastions with the last in line, Martinengo Bastion, collecting the adjacent walls into a huge spearhead plan form. It is a massive construction and proved impregnable to the Turks. The walls are 6m thick in places. Here, the angular corners were not rounded off, and double cannon posts were built into the walls.

The north wall was defended by the Del Mozzo and Diamante bastions. Turning seawards the small Signoria Bastion is passed and the famous citadel, or Othello's Tower, is reached

To the south of the tower is the Sea Gate (Porta del Mare), complete with the remains of an iron portcullis and iron clad doors built by the Ottoman Turks. In Venetian times the sea came right up to the gate. The stone lion is not another badge of Venice, more probably it is a simple medieval sculpture.

From this point, a long stretch of wall extends to the Djamboulat, or Arsenal Gate and Bastion in the city's southeast corner. It is here that the Turkish General Djamboulat Bey died in the siege. It seemed he committed a great suicidal act of bravery which opened the way for his men to enter the gate. For this he was martyred and buried within the bastion, a tomb being erected over his resting-place which is now a place of pilgrimage for Turks. The precincts leading off the gate were converted to a museum in 1968.

The Turks made vigorous attempts to breach the defences of this gate and until recently the area was a treasure trove of cannon balls and bits of metal.

From here to the Land Gate, the bastions of Camposanto, Andruzzi and Santa Napa punctuate the southern wall.

Caution should be taken on the wall for there are many unguarded openings and dangerous drops.

The Lion of St Mark, a medieval sculpture, set in the Venetian walls at Famagusta

The city walls of Famagusta, littered with cannon balls from seiges

The Siege of Famagusta

Famagusta was a fortified town long before the Venetians came to Cyprus. However, the increasing use of gunpowder in the Middle Ages had completely changed the style of warfare. In 1490 they set about remodelling and strengthening the walls. The ramparts were reduced in height and increased in thickness. Gun ports were built into the walls and all the angular corners were rounded off to deflect cannon balls. Famagusta became one of the strongest fortified cities in the Middle East. Even so, the efforts of the Venetians in the end proved to be of no avail, for the Turks broke through in 1571. Nevertheless, it had taken 10 months of terrible siege tactics and as many as 50,000 Turkish soldiers perished against 6,000 Venetians and Greeks. Marcantonio Bragadino, the Venetian commander was obliged to meet with the Turk Mustafa Pasha. Mustafa promptly had him flayed alive and his skin stuffed and paraded around the town.

A gateway at the Selimiye Mosque, Nicosia, reminiscent of another age

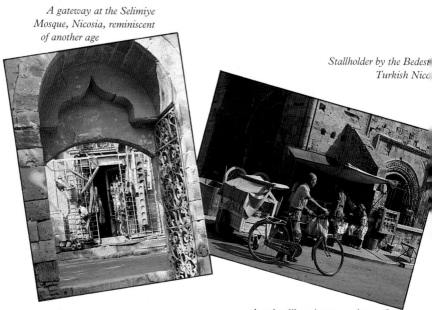

Stallholder by the Bedest *Turkish Nico*

A rocket-like minaret on Arasta Street, Nicosia, is a reminder that the populace is predominantly Muslim

Siskebap at a Kyrenia restaurant

Life in the North

Northern Cyprus within sight of the shores of Asia Minor is unmistakably eastern. The muezzin calls the faithful to prayer, although it may well be that the mosque was a Christian church many centuries before. However, the Turkish Cypriots today are not fervent about their religion. Their language is, of course, Turkish, although not the purer form, for it is a dialect with several local words.

Life has an easy pace, it may even have slipped back a little in time since the turmoil of 1974. Certainly there is little evidence of the frenetic holiday activity that characterises the rest of the island.

Patrons enjoy a harbourside drink in the sun, Kyrenia

Nevertheless, tourism is an important foreign currency earner. Agriculture is another, with citrus, vegetable and grain production being of greatest importance. In the towns people do their shopping in bazaars, and all around the noises of street trading can be heard. Hand carts stacked high with fresh fruit go rolling along the narrow streets and if two should meet, then the way is blocked for minutes while the vendors convey the traditional greetings.

On a national holiday the village coffee shops will be more crowded than usual. The all-male clientele will sit and gossip. Foreign visitors are rare and if passing are likely to be hailed and encouraged to sit down. The rules and courtesies of hospitality, so much a part of life in the Middle East, are not to be waived. A Turkish coffee will be offered, and there is no ambiguity here about its name as there is in the south, and it must be accepted. The same applies to the strong Turkish cigarette proffered with it. Little English is spoken in the villages but the gestures come thick and fast and the interpreter, perhaps a pressed man, will have to work overtime.

NORTH OF FAMAGUSTA

APOSTOLOS VARNAVAS

The monastery was built in honour of the apostle when a sepulchre containing his remains and a copy of the Gospel of Matthew in Barnabas' handwriting were found on the site in AD478.

Nothing remains of the original structure apart from a foundation and a marble column. Much of the destruction is attributed to Arab raiders. The present building was erected in the 18th century. Inside are life-size frescos painted in recent times, depicting scenes of the granting of independence to the Church of Cyprus in AD431. A custodian will show people round the church.
Location: 13km northwest of Famagusta. Open: 9am–1.30pm and 4.30pm–6.30pm, Tuesday to Saturday; October to May 8am–1pm and 2.30pm–5pm.

ENKOMI-ALASIA

The ruins of this Late Bronze Age city lie on the north bank of the Pedhaios river. This extensive collection of holes in the ground is of great significance to the archaeological history of Cyprus. The earliest remains date from the 17th century BC and suggest that the city was once the capital of Cyprus. It prospered through the export of copper and trade with Syria. In the 16th century BC Mycenaean craftsmen came to the city to produce vases and a ceramic industry evolved. Three hundred years later there was an influx of Achaean settlers. Unfortunately, much of the city was destroyed by a great fire, and subsequent earthquakes in the 12th century BC levelled much of what remained. Recovery was impossible and within 100 years Enkomi–Alasia was abandoned, the people moving to nearby Salamis.

Originally the site was considered to be no more than a necropolis, then in 1896 a British Museum Expedition discovered a number of tombs containing gold, ivory and pottery of the Mycenaean period. Later discoveries included the famous clay tablet of Cypro-Minoan script and in 1950 the Horned God of the 12th century BC, a priceless bronze figure now in the Cyprus Museum.

Visitors should start at the North Gate and proceed south to visit the **Sanctuary of the Horned God** followed by **Building 18**, the **House of the Pillar** and the **House of the Bronzes.** The latter is the remains of a 12th-century BC stone building found piled high with bronze objects.
Location: 8km north of Famagusta. Open: normally 7 days. Admission charge.

The easterly view from Kantara Castle

The formidable walls of Kantara Castle, perched menacingly on the hills of Kyrenia

KANTARA CASTLE

The castle's origins rest in Byzantine times, but it was the Lusignans who built the great ramparts, to complete Cyprus's northern chain of defences. Its stature is less than that of its sisters Buffavento and St Hilarion but it is no less splendid for that. The castle dominates the northern shore and looks out over the Kirpasa towards Asia Minor. To the south is the magnificent sweep of Famagusta Bay.

Much of the interior lies in ruins but the formidable outer wall is practically intact. Entrance is gained through a ruined barbican with twin towers, followed by a climb up some steps to reach a vaulted room. Opposite is the southeast tower with its vaulted guard quarters and cistern below. By proceeding along the south wall a tour in a clockwise direction is commenced. On the left is a barracks, complete with slit windows and a latrine showing the vestiges of a complex flushing system. More ruined chambers are passed as the path leads on to the final ascent. A room with Gothic windows marks the highest vantage point.

Location: 4km northeast of Kantara village; 38km north of Famagusta. Open normally 7 days. Admission free.

KARPAS PENINSULA

Also known as the 'Panhandle', this unique land formation has ancient ruins and secluded beaches hidden along its unspoilt shores. At the very eastern extremity is the monastery of Apostolos Andreas.

Location: northeast Cyprus.

The recently discovered ruins of the Salamis theatre

SALAMIS

This is the most impressive and important archaeological site in Cyprus.

The ruins are in two distinct sections separated by the main road. To the west is a necropolis with several intriguing tombs; to the east the ancient city itself. Three groups of ruins can be identified. Close to the main road is the Roman agora and the Temple of Zeus. Over on

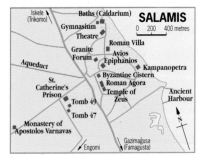

the east is the Kampanopetra and the ancient harbour. To the north is the gymnasium, baths and theatre. It is from the gymnasium area that the tour described below commences. It should be appreciated that the distance from the gymnasium to the Temple of Zeus is no less than 900m.

The columns of the **gymnasium** are plainly visible. Many are not from the original building at all, but from the nearby theatre, having been transferred during the Byzantine reconstruction of Salamis. These columns were re-erected in the 1950s.

From here we reach the main building of the **baths**, the *caldarium,* where the water was heated from underground furnaces off the adjoining north hall. Some restored mosaics can be seen in what is called the south hall. Ninety metres to the south is the impressive Roman **theatre**, discovered in 1959. Most of what can be seen has been reconstructed. It was probably built at the end of the 1st century AD, only to be destroyed by earthquakes during the 4th century.

Continuing south, the remains of a Roman villa are passed and turning left along the road a Byzantine **cistern** is found. Inside are paintings and inscriptions but access is by courtesy of the custodian as it is kept locked. Further south is the **Kampanopetra**, a large Early Christian basilica, only partially excavated. The **ancient harbour** is a few hundred metres ahead. Back on the metalled road, beyond the crossroads, is the **Granite Forum** where huge columns of impressive dimensions lie on the site. A little further to the south are the barely discernible remains of a second basilica, **Ayios Epiphanios**, dating from the 4th century.

If the road is followed round to the right the **vouta** is reached. This is a 7th-century cistern, or reservoir, that received water from Kythrea, 56km away, via an aqueduct. Close by is the **agora**, dating from the times of Ceasar Augusta and measuring 230m by 55m. At the far end, a few stones mark the site of the **Temple of Zeus**.

From here it is a short distance to

The clearly visible columns of the Roman Gymnasium at Salamis

the main road and then on to the western half of the site. A few hundred metres along the road is the **royal necropolis**. Several tombs can be found, described mainly by numbers although some have names. By the side of the road is tomb 50, St Catherine's Prison, built in Roman times but standing above tombs of the 7th century BC. Other tombs are numbers 47 and 49, both having skeletons of horses cast in the concrete floor.

Location: 9.5km north of Famagusta. Open: 9am–1.30pm and 4.30pm–6.30pm; October to May 8am–1pm and 2.30pm–5pm. Admission charge.

The City of Salamis

Salamis was a city kingdom, its exact date of origin unknown. However, various artefacts discovered on the site date from 11th century BC. Salamis rapidly became the most influential of the kingdoms of Cyprus and remained so for over a 1,000 years.

The kings of Salamis resisted the encroachments of the Persians and then the Ptolemies of Egypt. They were only partially successful in their defence but Salamis still continued as an important commercial centre under the Romans, although severe earthquakes in AD76 and AD77 caused much damage. There was no respite from natural calamities and in the 4th century earthquakes and tidal waves left Salamis in ruins. A new city was commissioned which survived until the 7th century.

The city lay beneath the sands for centuries and it was not until 1880 that the first excavations took place.

KYRENIA

DECORATIVE ARTS MUSEUM

The museum exhibits oil paintings, handicrafts from the Far East, and European and Chinese porcelain.
Location: Pasabahçe Sokagi (tel: 081 52142). Open: 9am–1.30pm and 4.30pm–6.30pm, Tuesday to Saturday; October to May 8am–1pm and 2.30pm–5pm. Admission charge.

FOLK ART MUSEM

The building itself is a model of an 18th-century Greek Cypriot house. Various

The harbour at Kyrenia with its fortifications that so often saved the town from piracy

handmade objects, pieces of 18th-century furniture and the implements used to make them, are displayed.
Location: by the harbour (tel: 081 52142). Open: 9am–1.30pm and 4.30pm–6.30pm, Tuesday to Saturday; October to May 8am–1pm and 2.30pm–5pm. Admission charge.

KYRENIA (GIRNE) CASTLE

A castle has stood on this waterfront site for centuries. Certainly the Byzantines built a fort, maybe as long ago as the 7th century. The Lusignans extended it and then the Venetians re-modelled it completely creating what we see today. The huge cylindrical bastion that pushes out into the harbour is their work.

Lusignan kings regularly stayed in the

Kyrenia's idyllic waterfront

castle and it was here that Eleanor of Aragon, the jealous wife of Peter I, had his mistress Jeanne Laleman imprisoned.

In more recent times it was used as a prison by the British until it became the responsibility of the Department of Antiquities.

From the entrance the main route leads directly from the gatehouse to the main courtyard, passing a narrow passage leading to a 12th-century Byzantine chapel.

The northwest tower should be examined before proceeding to the courtyard. Here, at the entrance, is the tomb of Sadik Pasha, the Turkish admiral to whom the castle was surrendered in 1570 by the Venetians. The **Shipwreck Museum** is found on the east side and must be visited for its priceless exhibit of the Kyrenia ship. Across the courtyard to the west are the royal apartments, although not very well preserved. Below are dungeons.

The battlements are accessible from the northwest tower and from here the panorama of the Kyrenia Hills is superb. No less remarkable is the view over the harbour. Walking along the walls requires care as there are unguarded drops everywhere. From the north wall the eastern ramparts can be reached, or a descent made through various

chambers to the courtyard.

The southwest tower is entered from the battlements. A passage leads down to the angular bastion and along the west wall, back to the courtyard entrance. *Location: the waterfront (tel: 081 52142). Open: 9am–1.30pm and 4.30pm–6.30pm, Tuesday to Saturday; October to May 8am–1pm and 2.30pm–5pm. Admission charge.*

KYRENIA SHIP

This is the oldest vessel ever to be recovered from the sea. It was wrecked in shallow waters less than 1.5km from the anchorage of Kyrenia. Lifting the wreck was effected during the summers of 1968 and 1969 by a team from the University of Pennsylvania. So delicate was the work that it was another six years before it was re-assembled. The wooden hull was made of Aleppo pine and measured 14m long by 4.5m across, and carried a single sail. The ship could make 4.5 knots and when it sank it was already about 80 years old. The cargo consisted of more than 400 wine amphorae from Rhodes, jars of almonds and 29 millstones. It is likely that the crew numbered no more than four.

To keep the timber in good condition the atmosphere of the museum is strictly controlled. *Location: Kyrenia Castle. Open: castle hours. Admission charge.*

LUSIGNAN TOWERS

Kyrenia was once a walled town, fortified by the Lusignans against attack from land and sea. Some of the towers built into the wall have survived. There is one by the harbour and the foundations of another by the customs house. The most intact of the towers is on Hurriyet Caddesi near the market.

WEST OF KYRENIA

AKHIROPIITOS MONASTERY

Since its foundation in the 12th century the monastery has undergone many alterations, being rebuilt in the 14th century and later acquiring a large apse.
Location: by the sea on Akhiropiitos Point, north of Alsancak (see also Lambousa). There are currently difficulties of access because of the military.

ANTIPHONITIS CHURCH

The outside looks a little neglected but is substantially as it used to be before the Turks took over northern Cyprus in 1974. From the central octagonal plan a dome of red tiles is carried on four columns and four piers. To the south, the 15th-century verandah is in disrepair. The priceless church interior has been extensively vandalised, resulting in the placement of new thick wooden doors, to prevent further desecration.
Locaton: 29km east of Kyrenia, via the track from Esentepe.

AYIOS MAMAS MONASTERY

The monastery is in the sizeable town of Guzelyurt, a tortuous maze of narrow streets and alleys.

The monastery was founded in Byzantine times, but nothing remains from this period. Extensive rebuilding was carried out in the 15th century, some of which still survives. However, a substantial portion of the present construction was added in two separate periods during the 18th century.

Inside the church the iconostasis is of various styles, the lower panels displaying fine examples of Venetian craftsmanship. Some of the wall paintings are particularly accomplished. A recess in the north wall is the tomb of Ayios Mamas himself.

Access is by courtesy of the custodian of the small **Museum of Archaeology and Natural History** next door. This, which is open office hours and has an admission charge, includes bronze artefacts, hellenistic pottery and a 4,000-year-old statue.
Location: Guzelyurt, 37km west of Nicosia (tel: 071 42202 museum). Open: museum 9am–1pm and 4.30pm–6.30pm, Tuesday to Saturday; October to May 8am–1pm and 2.30pm–5pm.

BELLAPAIS ABBEY

The precise origins of the abbey are not clear, but it is known that it was founded in the 13th century by Augustinian canons. The Latin kings of Cyprus supported the canons and Hugh III went as far as bestowing upon the abbot the privilege of wearing the mitre and golden spurs. The good times came to a sudden end in 1570 when the Turks destroyed much of the complex. The abbey deteriorated and not until 1912 were serious attempts made at restoration.

In the forecourt is the church, the earliest surviving part of the complex. Access is not usually offered by the custodian but may be on request. The interior is a Frankish Gothic design with a nave, two aisles, a north and south transept, and chancel. Access to the dormitory is by a night stair, and to the west a spiral stair continues to the roof providing a magnificent view of the Kyrenia Hills. Back in the forecourt a doorway leads to the centrepiece of Bellapais, the cloister with its tall dark cypress trees. Although a ruin, with the arches of the arcade to the west having lost their vaults, it is an impressive place with fine Gothic detailing. In the northwest corner lies a large marble sarcophagus and lavabo where monks washed their hands before entering the refectory. This splendid vaulted hall is unequalled in Cyprus. On the east side is a rose window, and a staircase within the thickness of one wall rises up to the pulpit. Six windows in the north wall reveal a magnificent view over the coast.

East of the cloister is the chapter house and an undercroft, complete with the stone benches used by the canons. On the same level is a vaulted treasury.

Location: 6.5km southeast of Kyrenia. Open: 9am–1.30pm and 4.30pm–6.30pm, Tuesday to Saturday; October to May 8am–1pm and 2.30pm–5pm. Admission charge.

The impressive Gothic arches of Bellapais Abbey

Bellapais Abbey, nestling in the lower slopes of the Kyrenian hills

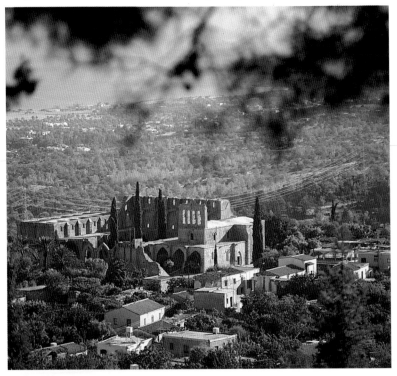

BUFFAVENTO

This is not the best preserved of the three great elevated castles of the northern mountains, but at 790m above sea-level it is the highest.

During the winter months the cold Anatolian wind can blow a sharp reminder that the Italian name of the castle means 'blown by the wind'. Not much is known of the castle's detailed history but it certainly existed in the 12th century. A garrison was in occupation until well into the Venetian period, but ironically the last few years of this foreign domination saw the castle dismantled and left to the elements.

From the remains of the gatehouse a long flight of worn steps leads up the high crag, passing the chambers of the lower ward which was constructed over a vaulted water system. Further steps lead to the upper ward and the remains of a chapel. The visitor can go no further for all around the land falls away and the panorama is breathtaking, leaving no doubts as to why the Lusignans chose such a site.

Location: 13km southeast of Kyrenia. For those without a jeep the last 2.5km must be made on foot from above the village of Gungor.

LAMBOUSA

Over the years the site has been occupied by Greeks, Phoenicians, Ptolemies, Romans and Byzantines as well as being one of the Hittite or city kingdoms of Cyprus. In pre-Christian times Lambousa was a major exporter of pottery. Little remains today, although the Roman fish tanks with their inlet and outlet channels have survived, and the supports to their sluice gates are still in position. Early this century the Lambousa Treasure, including several silver plates from the 7th century, was unearthed. Much of it is preserved in the Cyprus Museum.

Location: on the shore west of Kyrenia, 1.5km from Karavas. (See also **Akhiropiitos Monastery.**) *Access is currently difficult because of the military.*

LEFKA

The town has been inhabited by Turkish Cypriots for more than 400 years and has an authentic Turkish atmosphere.

Location: 52km west of Nicosia.

Buffavento Castle sitting precariously in the northern mountains on a site deliberately choosen for its natural defences

The craggy heights of St Hilarion Castle

ST HILARION

The castle may have been named after St Hilarion the Great, the founder of monasticism in Palestine, or a later St Hilarion from the Holy Land.

Whatever the truth the Byzantines built a church here in the 10th century in memory of a St Hilarion. It developed into a monastery and soon became fortified. During the Lusignan reign the fortifications were strengthened with the construction of strong outer walls. After the occupation of Cyprus by the Venetians in 1489, however, the new administration ordered the dismantling of St Hilarion along with Buffavento and Kantara castles.

Once through the entrance the visitor will see a restored gatehouse and on the left a barbican. By the south wall is a cistern and further on the stables. An ascent to the next level brings some fine views of the walls and a semi-circular tower. From this position the middle ward is entered to reach the 10th-century Byzantine church at the top of the stairs.

Steps descend to a vaulted passage and a hall that may have been a refectory; the passage leads on to a belvedere with adjacent kitchens. The accommodation to the northeast was for the royal family. Today this is a restaurant.

The upper ward is a separate entity, reached by a path from the middle ward. It is a stiff climb to the highest level and in summer this is a thirsty undertaking.

At a good height an ascent to the left of the main route leads to St John's Tower, sheer on three sides, from where a Prince of Antioch hurled his enemies.

Regaining the main route, paths and steps lead on through an arched gateway. The Queen's Window has side seats and, although it has lost much of its tracery, it retains a marvellous view. *Location: 8km southeast of Kyrenia. Open: 9am–1.30pm and 4.30pm–6.30pm; October to May 8am–1pm and 2.30pm–5pm. Admission charge.*

Remains of the Roman mosaic floor at Soli

SOLI

The city was founded at the beginning of the 6th century BC and took its name in honour of Solon, the Athenian statesman who came to Cyprus in his old age. It prospered and became one of the ten city kingdoms of Cyprus, playing an important role in the struggle against Persian domination. Near by were the copper mines of Skouriotissa and Mavrovouni, and with the arrival of the Romans Cyprus became a major copper exporter.

The Romans constructed the **theatre** on the hillside, possibly on the site of a smaller Greek one. Some 3,500 seats were built into the hillside, overlooking the sea. It was discovered in 1930 and subsequently restored. Much of the original stonework had been removed in the 18th century, some being used in the building of the Suez Canal. Only the floor of the orchestra and stage area is the original.

Lower down the hill is the **basilica**, built in the 5th century and abandoned after Arab raids in AD632. A small part of the mosaic floor has survived and the bird designs are of special interest. Over to the west is the **agora**, very little of which has survived.

It was at Soli that the famous marble statue of Aphrodite was found, now kept in the Cyprus Museum. To the west and just off shore is the island rock of Limnitis. During the excavations at Soli the Swedish archaeologists visited the island and discovered various pieces of pottery and tools from the Neolithic period.

Location: the southern shore of Guzelyurt Körfezi, 20km west of the town of Guzelyurt. Open: all times. Admission charge at certain hours.

VOUNI PALACE

The site is breath-taking, overlooking the sea from a high plateau. Inland the panorama is almost as spectacular. Excavations were first carried out between 1928 and 1929. Nothing earlier than the 5th century BC was uncovered, making the palace younger than anticipated. Nevertheless, there is good evidence that it was built by a pro-Persian king when parts of the island were in unsuccessful revolt against the Persians. The palace would serve to hold in check nearby Soli, which had sided with the rebels. Other evidence suggests the palace is of later origins, perhaps built after the revolt which set a pro-Greek dynasty in power around 300BC. We may never know the true story of Vouni's origins but it had a brief existence, being set alight in 380BC when the Persians regained control of Cyprus.

Little remains of the walls but it seems clear that there were several different distinct periods of construction.

The main entrance of the palace is approached from the southwest and passes into the megaron and royal apartments. Down a few steps is a peristyle court with surrounding rooms. In the centre of the court is a cistern and by the well-head a stone slab that would have at one time carried a windlass.

The water system of the palace was quite eleborate and designed to supply all the major rooms. Well-arranged baths were served by this complex plumbing and had a ready supply of hot and cold water. Some distance from the palace are various shrines and several interesting sculptures have been found close by. To the south, up on the high ground, is what little remains of the **Temple of Athena.**

Location: south of Guzelyurt Körfezi, 27km west of Guzelyurt. Open: all times. Admission charge at certain hours.

Visit the remains of Vouni Palace set in a spectacular landscape

Getting away from it all

SOUTH CYPRUS

CAMEL TRAIL

The trail runs from the high Troodos Mountains to the port of Paphos. To follow it along its length is rather an ambitious temptation. However, to meet up with it for half a day is still quite an experience.

The Venetians cut the route through the hills to improve trade and communications. Initially, copper from the Troodos mines was the main commodity.

Three rivers barred the way: a tributary of the Dhiarizos, the Dhiarizos itself, and the Xeros. This was not a problem to such master builders as the Venetians and they bridged them all. Elea Bridge is the furthest east, Kelephos is in the middle and Roudhias at the western end where the route starts to descend towards the coast.

The trail is unused today, although a dirt road approximates to it and carries the occasional vehicle. This suggested trip starts in the west at the village of Galataria. For safety and comfort a jeep is required, ground clearance being an important factor. A plentiful supply of liquid refreshment should be carried.

From the village the road to Kilinia should be taken and the start of the stony, but tolerable, road to the deserted village of Vrecha, 4km away. On nearing the centre, with its little memorial, the reason for the abandonment becomes quite clear, explained in an instant by the mosque and its battered minaret. This is a Turkish village and everybody left in 1974.

The way out of any Cypriot village is perplexing and escape from a deserted one borders on the impossible. At the time of printing the best choice of exit is to turn right at the memorial through some houses, down an atrocious road which, thankfully, quickly improves. A track to the right, leading to more buildings, should be ignored and soon after leaving the village take the next fork to the right. It is another 5km to the bridge which can be seen in the valley after about 4km.

This is a convenient place to stop and climb out on to the hillside. On a calm day the silence is as nowhere else, eerie, almost disturbing. There are no tourist motorbikes, just the marvellous view over the valley to great white cliffs, and the silence. In midsummer the heat on this southern slope is murderous; it is no place to break down or get stuck. Drivers should make no move forward they feel they may not be able to reverse. However, on the correct track, with common sense, there should be little trouble. In spring and autumn it may be an idea to park and walk down to the bridge; in summer, driving is the sensible choice.

Once by the bridge an immediate difficulty presents itself. A cursory examination of the Venetian edifice indicates that a laden camel would have the hardest of times crossing it. However, there are more pressing matters. What is much more important is to put on a pair of flip flops and wander down the Xeros river through the trees. In spring there may be too much water for this, in the summer there will be only a little. Within 250m a series of pools will be reached which have the clearest, purest and coolest water imaginable. Not a second should be lost in taking the plunge and if nothing else does, this will make the whole trip to Cyprus worthwhile.

Once fully restored, with a body temperature approaching normal, it will be easier to explore the river bed and its surrounding area, the enhanced senses being able to appreciate it to a greater extent. Intrepids may wish to continue the camel route to Kelephos Bridge, or even as far as Elea Bridge.

On a cautionary note, keep an eye open for snakes and avoid the river bed if a thunderstorm is raging up the valley in the Troodos.

The Camel Trail, an old Venetian trade route

Cape Arnouti, Cyrus's most westerly point

CAPE ARNOUTI

Geographically, the cape of western Cyprus is as remote as anywhere on the island with a road that peters out some 9km to the east. Therefore, most explorers of this stretch of coast might expect to have it to themselves. That this is not the case is attributable to one thing – the motorbike. Many of today's visitors to Cyprus have the skill, even with a pillion, to traverse the bumpy track, with ruts deeper than can be imagined, from the Baths of Aphrodite all the way to the cape.

So perhaps not unreasonably, one has to share this magnificent territory with a few others. And of course, now there is a choice of how the visitor can get there. One can join the 'bikeys' and risk the bumps and a possible plummet into the sea from a great height or make enquiries to share or hire a jeep. Walking there and back (18km) will not appeal to everybody, and would be more than an exhausting punishment in summer. The answer for foot travellers is to go to Lachi and find a boatman, and ask to be taken to the cape or part way along the peninsula, and hike back. It is essential to leave the car at the Baths of Aphrodite

and be picked up from the beach there, otherwise the walking is extended by 4.5km. Speedboats do the trip in 20 minutes, and the costs can be reduced by sharing with another party. Boat travellers should appreciate that disembarkation can be a leap and a splash.

Specific destinations are irrelevant in this wonderful area. The cape itself is fine enough, but low lying and rocky it is no place for a swim, although an ideal spot for a picnic. A little to the east some shelves in the rock seem ideal for sunbathing. Around the cape to the south are dramatic-looking sea cliffs, though sufficiently distant to discourage thoughts of exploration.

On leaving the cape walkers have to decide between the easy inland track or the shore, the ground in between being a mass of impenetrable bushes. It is a fascinating landscape; the rocks are white, the soil deep red and the sea a tempting blue. To the south, a church stands silhouetted on the hills of the Akamas. A detour through the bush might disturb a hare, but only a silver flash will be seen.

Twenty minutes after leaving the cape two coastal wrecks will be reached. They appear to have met their unfortunate end some time ago and now provide a refuge for countless species of marine life.

Although the cape is now behind, the panorama ahead more than makes up for it. The shore line is never less than wonderful and the unusual flat-topped hill of Vakinoes stands magnificent in the middle distance. Now is perhaps the time to seek out a secluded cove and try the cool waters. There is, however, no hurry, for it is more or less the same all the way to distant Ayios Yeoryios Island. Certainly the land turns from red to white and one may be passed by a bike or two, or a truck full of goats, but things are hardly the worse for this.

It does come as something of a surprise to realise that this part of the Akamas is an artillery range for the British Army. Large red signs make this absolutely clear and warn walkers to keep well away from the red flags and not to touch objects on the ground 'as they may explode and kill you'! The long march to the Baths of Aphrodite allows time to ponder on the fate of this unique part of Cyprus, and whether a firing range will ever be exchanged for a coastline of hotels.

The view of Cape Arnouti from the Baths of Aphrodite is one of tranquil beauty

Village Life

Understandably, the old ways are changing in many parts of Cyprus, but there are more than 300 villages on Cyprus where traditional ways of life continue. Broadly speaking, Cypriot villages all seem to have the same plan, narrow roads and tracks converging into a central square.

The Men

The café is the fulcrum of the village, at least for the men. It is frequented at all times. There is always plenty to be said, whether it is complaints at the price of olives or the inclement weather.

Coffee is the preferred drink, a minute quantity being served with a glass of water. The custom is to make it last. Later in the day, many switch over to brandy. Tavali or backgammon are favourite pastimes and you will usually find a cut-throat game in progress.

Village women are clearly excluded from all this but foreigners, male or female, are welcome. After the first curious glances the visitors may well be left alone, but there may be an attempt to draw them into conversation. This is unlikely to be in English, but non-Greek or Turkish speakers should not be deterred, there is something about Cypriot coffee shops that makes this ignorance almost irrelevant, especially after the inevitable outsize brandy.

The Women

So what are the village women doing? It could well be that they do all the work, for even women of very mature years are seen on the outskirts of the village looking after the fields or tending donkeys piled high with straw and grasses.

The men would undoubtedly point out, however, that they are early risers and have finished work by the time the tourist is taking his breakfast: first light comes early to Cyprus's clear skies. They might also say that a visit to a shady back street will find their wives relaxing with their embroidery and knitting.

The quietness of the villages in the afternoon is always striking. One reason for this is that many young people leave to find work in the towns and resorts, only coming back at the weekend when there will be a big gathering with all the family. At other times the village comes to life for a cheese or flower festival. A bandstand will be erected and on the appointed day friends and relatives from the surrounding area gather to eat, drink and dance into the early hours.

A tense game of
Tavali in progress

A shepherdess
with her flock in
the Avgas Gorge,
near Ayios
Yeoryios

...e village priest, Pano
...anayia

Village craftsman and his
copper wares

The habitually happy
...atures of a cypriot face

CEDARS VALLEY

Despite much publicity this valley in the western Troodos is not overrun with tourists. Few people set out for the cedars and even less get there. An explanation is its isolation and a twisting and turning dirt road leading to it which at first sight seems to offer a good chance of getting the traveller lost.

In reality, a visit to Cedars Valley is the high spot of a trip through the cool western forest. If the cedars are found, then so much the better

The cedars *(Cedrus likami)* are native to Cyprus and grow to a great height. They flourish at altitudes ranging from 1,000 to 1,400m.

Those with four-wheel drive will be able to make fast progress on the forest tracks, which in many sections are reasonably smooth. However, ordinary cars could have problems and should stick to clearly signposted routes and turn back if the road deteriorates.

CRUISES FROM LARNACA

There are boat trips to Larnaca Bay and Ayia Napa from the marina area and the small harbour at the south end of the town. Ayia Napa is no less than 37km distant, a long way and requiring precautions against sunburn.

CRUISE TO LARA BEACH

The beach is no longer undiscovered but a visit by boat from Paphos is still a wonderful day out for those that enjoy boat trips in the sun. At 25km, it takes a long time and again precautions should be taken against sunburn.

There are two beaches (see page 97), one on either side of the headland, where the splendour of the sand and sea matches the views of the Akamas Hills. A turtle hatchery provides alternative entertainment.

Lush Cedars Valley in the Troodos Mountains, a paradise off the beaten track

Yermasoyia Dam, a popular picnic spot

CYPRUS'S DAMS

Cyprus has several picturesque dams, some of which furnish splendid picnic spots.

The dam above Yermasoyia, near Limassol, is a renowned favourite. A more recent construction, east of Paphos by the village of Phinikas, is twice as big and picnic possibilities exist on numerous stretches of the bank.

Evretou Dam, off the Paphos Polis road near Skoulli, is another recent development, and is well worth the 2km dirt-track detour off the main road.

GHOST CITY OF FAMAGUSTA

There are cruises from the harbour of Ayia Napa, that pass around Cape Greco to Fig Tree Bay, and head up the coast to stand off and peer at the new city of Famagusta shimmering in the distance. Unlike the old walled city of Famagusta, the new city is completely closed to visitors and Cypriots. There are not too many deserted cities in the world so this trip is quite special.

The distance from Ayia Napa is 16km and again protection against the sun is required.

Those who are not good sailors but want to see the city can take one of the trips by taxi or minibus that visit selected villages near Ayia Napa and then go on to a viewing platform at Dherinia to see the deserted town through telescopes and binoculars.

Admiring the beauty of the Cypriot coastline from a cruise boat

PAPOUTSA

Papoutsa's height of 1,554m above sea-level in the eastern Troodos is more than respectable and no roads run to its rocky summit. Olympus does its best to block out the view to the west but even so the panorama is amazing. Cars can be left on the high pass where the road from Palekhori to Ayios Theodhoros is met by the one from Agros. Papoutsa is the peak to the southeast, the ridge of which runs right down to the pass.

The ascent does not entail hours of foot slogging. The hill can be rushed in 25 minutes or taken at a more leisurely 45. The ridge is easy walking, although every step is uphill. There are some fine specimens of dried flowers – dead but still in the ground – on these heights.

The summit is something of a surprise; a large cross and a stone shelter are more reminiscent of northern European hills than Cyprus.

Undiscovered stretches of sandy beach at Pomos Point

POMOS POINT TO KATO PYRGOS

The beaches on this stretch of coast, east of Khrysokhou Bay in western Cyprus, are still mostly quiet and undiscovered. There are two or three good stretches of sand before progress eastwards is abruptly halted by the military

surrounding the isolated Turkish enclave of Kokkina. To regain the shore it is necessary to detour 11km up and then down the mountainside. This frustration is offset somewhat by the splendid views.

Down again on the coast, the road eventually reaches Kato Pyrgos. The village is of no great merit but provides an excellent lunchtime stop. It is, of course, literally the end of the line, being the western extremity of the military division of Cyprus.

WINE VILLAGES

Cyprus has suddenly gained a new region to go with its Marathasa, Pitsilia, Solea and Tilliria. It is the Krassochoria (the wine villages), found in the southwest Troodos, 32km from Limassol.

The main villages are **Omodhos**, **Pakhna** and **Arsos**. They are not too far apart and all can be reached on metalled roads. Old traditions have survived where cultivation of the vineyards and wine-making are still the main occupation of most of the inhabitants. The product of their efforts is a dry red wine. In Omodhos an old farmhouse has been restored, complete with wine press.

NORTH CYPRUS

BESPARMAK MOUNTAIN (PENTADAKTYLOS)

The Greek name Pentadaktylos means 'five fingers' and indeed the mountain has at least five unusual spikey summits.

Cars should be left at the top of the pass, 16km southeast of Kyrenia, where a path runs along the south face and from which the rocky peaks are plainly visible. One can simply admire the features of the ridge from here and watch the griffon vultures alighting on the inaccessible pinnacles or climb the lower slopes until the going gets hard. The place is teeming with vipers, so care is needed where feet and hands åre placed.

GUZELYURT BAY

There is approximately 40km of this western shore, much of it sandy, with no hotels. Access is poor; one route being through Guzelyurt itself and then through Yayla on a variety of road surfaces.

Another possibility is further to the north via Akdeniz and on to the shore by the Bronze Age site of **Paleokastro**. It is found on a hill overlooking the sea. An intriguing collection of over 2,000 earthenware male figures, discovered here, are now in the Cyprus Museum in Nicosia.

KARPAS (KIRPASA)

The one sure place to get away from it all in Cyprus is the Karpas Peninsula, for it is a long way from the main towns. It is an unusual land formation, nearly 80km long and 11km wide. From Nicosia or Kyrenia the traveller will be weary before the start of the peninsula is reached. Famagusta is a better setting out point.

On the whole, the road keeps clear of the coast with occasional roads and tracks to the sea. There are ancient sites on both shores. **Galounia** is the first on the north side and perhaps this was the town of ancient Aphrodision.

There are several small bays and inlets along the coast until Cape Apostolos Andreas, where the ancient site of **Kastros** is reached together with the journey's end.

On the south side of the peninsula the rocky shore occasionally gives way to sandy dunes and a shallow sea.

A sandy bay on the southern shores of the Karpas Peninsular

Shopping

Cyprus is not exactly the shopping capital of Europe, and those who stick to the shops in tourist resorts may despair of ever being able to find anything other than a 'Cyprus is for lovers' T-shirt or a pair of luminous sunglasses.

There are, however, other places to look and other things to buy. Focus in particular on locally made goods; pottery, jewellery, basketware, lace and embroidery.

An oddity which might not immediately spring to mind to buy is spectacles. There are many qualified opticians in Cyprus and they can supply glasses within 24 hours at much cheaper prices than at home. Many now offer a special tourist service. Note that half-day closing is on the Wednesday.

SOUTHERN CYPRUS

GREEK NICOSIA
Ledra Street and Onasagoras Street
These two narrow streets are the focus of the old town. There are many clothes and shoe shops catering mainly for local trade but visitors may be able to pick up bargains and, unlike in many Mediterranean countries, the clothes on sale are modern in style.

Towards the bottom of the streets is a profusion of material shops with their rolls of cloth crowding the already narrow pavements. In some of these are tailors who make suits to order.

Leather goods make a popular souvenir

Laiki Yitonia, an area restored to create the atmosphere of old Nicosia

Laiki Yitonia
Laiki Yitonia is a restored district which tries to evoke the atmosphere of old Nicosia. There are many tourist shops, some of which sell better than average souvenirs. Try here for jewellery, cloth, rugs and pottery.

There is one good bookshop and several places to buy leather goods, including shoes, handbags and suitcases. The area is particularly pleasant to walk around and there are plenty of cafés and restaurants at which to rest and watch the world go by.

The New Town and Archbishop Makarios III Avenue

This broad avenue has a completely different ambience, pursuing a sophisticated image. There are plenty of expensive jewellery shops as well as sports retailers selling even more expensive trainers and tracksuits. Two very modern shopping plazas have recently been completed with escalators, mirrors and marble floors.

At the end of the avenue is Woolworths, the first departmemt store to open in Cyprus. It has now been followed by Marks & Spencer and British Home Stores, but Woolworths retains its allure and seems to be permanently busy, full of excited Cypriots.

Other areas

The **Cyprus Handicraft Centre** at the east end of Athalassa Avenue has craftsmen at work with their products on sale. (It is too far to walk from the city centre.)

LARNACA
Zinonos Kitieos Street

This is the main shopping district of Larnaca. There is a mixture of shops selling the standard tourist goods as well as clothes shops catering for local residents. These include a Marks & Spencer in familiar colours but looking out of place in this eastern street.

The seafront

There are a few souvenir shops and a couple of small supermarkets, but mainly the seafront is occupied by cafés and pubs.

LIMASSOL

The hotels stretch for many miles east of Limassol, and where there are hotels in Cyprus there are always tourist shops and supermarkets. All the necessary day-to-day items can be bought here, as well as the standard souvenirs.

In the town itself, Ayiou Andreou Street is the best way to reach the shopping area. At its far western end, built into several arches near the castle, is a small shopping arcade containing up-market boutiques and a jewellery shop.

On **Ayiou Andreou Street** itself there is a large number of cloth merchants and shops selling leatherware, mainly handbags and suitcases. As in the other towns there are plenty of shoe retailers. Rough and ready leather sandals are very cheap and widely available, but tend to disintegrate if exposed to rainy weather.

There is a Marks & Spencer amidst several other clothes shops and the Mavros shopping arcade has the usual variety of establishments.

On the seafront, a number of shops sell copper goods and some high-quality pottery.

Larnaca's Marks & Spencer shop, incongruous in its Cypriot setting

Tourist shops in Paphos

PAPHOS
Lower Town

This is where the tourist shops are gathered in abundance. Where Apostolou Pavlou Avenue joins the seafront are several jewellery shops. Then turning left along the shoreline, away from the harbour, is a series of shops selling what can only be described as junk. The more discerning should move on to an area of shops arranged around a courtyard, set back from the road, where there are several sculpture workshops offering something a little bit different, although with prices to match.

Upper Town

The upper town is a warren of busy streets, with only shops in the pedestrianised area focusing on the tourist. There is a good bookshop off to the right from Nikodimou Mylona Street, but otherwise the shops are standard establishments, selling clothes and shoes. Curiously, the most ubiquitous product in Paphos is the barbecue complete with a sophisticated set of turning skewers.

OTHER PLACES

Lefkara is the home of lace-making but visitors should be careful to ensure that they get the genuine article and not imitations. Lefkara lace is, however, sold all across the island.

Phini, Kornos and **Yeroskipos** have good pottery shops; especially for larger jars and flowerpots.

Basketware originates from **Liopetri** on the way to Ayia Napa, but is again widely available elsewhere.

FOOD SHOPPING

There are food stores everywhere in Cyprus. Visitors will have no trouble buying as they do at home.

The range and standard of .. ... in the supermarkets can sometimes be disappointing. The best places for fruit and vegetables are the markets or roadside fruit sellers. The quality of the latter is usually very high, the seller having usually grown it himself and they are quite likely to throw in an extra plum or two if they like the look of you. The roads up to the mountains are the best sources of such stalls.

Fruit and vegetable stall at Nicosia market

Girne Caddesi, Nicosia

NORTHERN CYPRUS

Isolated by the international community, the range of goods available in northern Cyprus is less than in the south. None the less, most of the staple goods are readily available.

Visitors should not expect large modern shops but a rather more bazaar-like atmosphere. Made-to-measure shoes are available to women with matching belt and handbag. Despite the island's partition, Lefkara lace from the south can be purchased.

Turkish Nicosia

The main shopping areas are **Girne Caddesi**, **Arasta** pedestrianised area and the **Galleria Arcade**.

On Girne Caddesi are some larger shops, banks and jewellers. Galleria, which comprises two storeys, has an abundance of sportswear shops.

The Arasta pedestrian area is the liveliest and most interesting place to explore. There are lots of material shops, including some where you can get a suit made. There are also carpenters and leather merchants all around the city. Otherwise, the main things to look for are jewellery, pottery and ornaments.

FAMAGUSTA (GAZIMAGUSA)

The streets leading to Lala Mustafa Pasha Mosque have some atmospheric old shops. Some specialise in attractive handknitted mohair sweaters, others in high-quality leather coats and bags. The usual range of ceramics and brassware is also available.

KYRENIA (GIRNE)

There are few shops to interest the visitor. Nevertheless, **Hurriyet Cadessi** has one or two traders selling handmade pottery and ceramics. Brass and copper products can also be found. Women may find some of the belts and handbags worth buying.

Entitlement

*T*here is little doubt that the holiday maker will have a very full and enjoyable visit. To make it all complete the Cypriots make sure there is a variety of evening entertainment. Many of the hotels have folk evenings and cabarets, the larger ones have resident bands for anyone wishing to dance their way through the evening.

In the resorts there are bars, tavernas and discotheques, the latter often being part of hotel complexes. Understandably, a big town like Limassol has much more to offer than, say, Larnaca or Paphos. At certain times in the evening there are so many youngsters milling around the discotheques that traffic can be brought to a standstill. To the west of the town there are wonderful summer performances of music and drama in the Roman theatre at Kourion.

In Ayia Napa, exclusively a holiday town, life goes on until the early hours and some people go straight from the night clubs to the beach. Kyrenia has a preponderance of casinos. Many simply house a collection of one-armed bandits and pin tables; however, at least two hotels have roulette and blackjack.

Many tavernas in the south have their own traditional dance group, and at some point in the evening visitors will be encouraged to take the floor *en masse* and join in, probably to the tune of *Zorba the Greek.*

Nicosia is not a resort town and special entertainment for visitors is rare. The municipal theatre stages plays in Greek and English, and also concerts. The British Council puts on various entertainments by visiting theatre companies and celebrities. There are, of course, nightclubs and bars.

What's on!

Time Out tourist and business guide is free and useful, as is the Cyprus Tourism Organisation's (CTO) guide of *Monthly Events.* Both these publications are available at hotels and tourist offices. Also of use are the CTO's annual *Diary of Events,* listing the entire year's holidays and organised activities, and CTO's *Traveller's Handbook.* These can be obtained from any CTO office in Cyprus and abroad.

From June to September a tourist radio programme called *Welcome to Cyprus* is broadcast on all days except Sunday. It is in several languages including English and is transmitted on 603KHz (498m). Information about weather, currency rates and cultural events is given out at 10.00am, 2.00pm and 7.30pm.

Greek dancers in Limassol

NICOSIA

CINEMAS
Metropol, *Theodotou St (tel: 02 444840)*.

CULTURAL CENTRES
British Council, *Museum St (tel: 02 442485)*. Puts on various entertainments by visiting theatre companies and celebrities.
Goethe Institute, *21 Markos Drakos Avenue (tel: 02 462608)*. Shows mainly German films, mostly Wednesday evenings.

DISCOTHEQUES
Amanda's Disco Club, *Stassinos St, Engomi district (tel: 02 366418)*.
Galaxy, *44 I Patatsou Street, Engomi district (tel: 02 458184)*. The biggest disco in Nicosia.

NIGHTCLUBS
Crazy Horse Cabaret, *Omirou Street (tel: 02 473569)*. European ballets, acrobats and magicians.
Erotico, *2 Athinas Avenue (tel: 02 434811)*.
Maxim Cabaret, *14 Zenas de Tyras Street (tel: 02 445679)*.

NIGHTSPOTS
Elysee, *Pantheon Building, Evagoras Avenue (tel: 02 473773)*. Bouzoukia.
Fraktis, *Nicosia/Limassol Road (tel: 02 424100)*. Bouzoukia
Isadoras, *1 Deligiorgis Street/Demis Severis Avenue (tel: 02 477387)*. Greek and pop music.
Palace, *116 Grivas Dhigenis Avenue (tel: 02 353976)*. Bouzoukia.
Varonos, *48d Grivas Dhigenis Avenue (tel: 02 443404)*.

PUBS AND BARS
Blinker Pub, *22a Papakyriakou Street, Makedonitissa (tel: 02 351550)*.
Corner Pub, *48 Demis Severis Avenue (tel: 02 465735)*.
Green Line Pub, *Athens Avenue, north of Famagusta Gate*. This is the place to drink in unique surroundings, for as the name indicates the pub is right on the Green Line.
Kalypso Pub, *56 Iphigenia Street, Acropolis (tel: 02 420470)*.
Maple Leaf Pub, *43 Galipolis Avenue, Lycavitos (tel: 02 473546)*.
Mythos Pub, *Th. Theodotou Street (tel: 02 452010)*.
Romylos Pub, *4 Zena Street (tel: 02 445376)*.

THEATRES
Municipal Theatre, *Museum Street (tel: 02 463028)*. Regular performances of classical music and plays.

SOUTH EAST

CINEMAS
Larnaca
Rex, *Democratia Sq (tel: 04 652223)*.

Dhekelia (Sovereign Base)
Key

CULTURAL CENTRES
Ayia Napa
Monastery Square, folk dances and songs every Sunday afternoon.

DISCOTHEQUES
Ayia Napa
Babylon, *Ayia Theklis Street (tel: 03 722666)*.
The Cave, *28 Kryo Nero Street (tel: 03 722306)*.
Larnaca
Cosmos, *37a Archbishop Makarios Avenue (tel: 04 629784)*. Oldest disco in Larnaca, all kinds of music.
Ecstasy, *Dhekalia Road (tel: 04 652432)*. Live music.
Pussy Cat, *32 Archbishop Makarios Avenue (tel: 04 622115)*.
Stringfellows, *Dhekalia Road (tel: 04 624157)*.
Venus, *Mackenzie Area (tel: 04 628666)*.
Xanadu's, *(tel: 04 624322)*. For all ages, 50's to 90's music.
Protaras
Amadeus Disco Nightclub, *near Sunrise Hotel*. Oldies music until 1pm.

NIGHTCLUBS
Ayia Napa
Black and White, *Seferi Square (tel: 03 721692)*.
Larnaca
Dandella, *Atlantis and Archbishop Makarios Avenue (tel: 04 620428)*. Floor show every night. Acrobats, magicians and oriental dancing.
Nostalgia, *3 General Timayia Avenue (tel: 04 636550)*. Music and floor show.

PUBS AND BARS
Ayia Napa
Pink Panther *(tel: 03 721437)*.
Rikkos *(tel: 03 721160)*.
Larnaca
Mayfair, *73 Athens Avenue (tel: 04 625966)*.
Meeting Pub, *1 Kosma Lyssioti (tel: 04 656893)*.

THEATRE
Larnaca
Open Air Amphitheatre, *Artemedos Avenue*. Greek drama during Larnaca festival (see page 62). Performances are on an *ad hoc* basis; the Tourist Office will have details.

SOUTH
CINEMA
Akrotiri (Sovereign Base)
Astra.
Limassol
Apollon, *10 Meskit St (tel: 05 365293)*.
Othellos, *Thessaloniki St (tel: 05 363811)*

CULTURAL CENTRES
Limassol
Town Hall *Arch Kyprianos St* (tel: 05 363103).
Films, videos and lectures in the evenings.
Michaelides Music School *(tel: 05 335155)*.
Classical music recitals by celebrated soloists.

DISCOTHEQUES
Limassol
Blow Up, *Georgiou Street, Potamos Yermasoyia (tel: 05 323127)*.
Caribbean Disco, *Georgiou Street, Potamos Yermasoyia (tel: 05 321868)*.
Images/Piccadilly, *Georgiou Street, Potamos Yermasoyia.*
90s Disco, *Amathus Area (tel: 05 322324)*.
Malibu Disco, *Ambelakion Street (tel: 05 322500)*.
Venus Disco Club, *90 Geogiou Street, Potamos Yermasoyia (tel: 05 321294)*. The only beach disco.
Whispers, *Georgiou Street, Potamos Yermasoyia (tel: 05 326464)*. Laser show.

NIGHTCLUBS
Limassol
Casba Cabaret, *32 Paul Mela Street (tel: 05 353817)*. Czechoslovakian orchestra. International floor show and striptease.
Celebrity, *Kanikos Street (tel: 05 368786)*.
Enter Club, *23 Andreas Street (tel: 05 377000)*. International show.
Felix, *Makarios III Avenue (tel: 05 338329)*.
Kit Kat, *17 Drousioti Street (tel: 05 346392)*.
Lido Nightclub, *20 Paul Mela Street (tel: 05 368598)*. European and Asian floorshows.
Playboy, *23a Drousioti Street (tel: 05 341786)*. European and Asian shows, bouzouki and jazz.
Zygos, *78 Makarios III Avenue (tel: 05 336129)*.

PUBS
Limassol
Cella, *Ay. Tychonas (tel: 05 322058)*.
Ship Inn, *28 Oct St (tel: 05 355180)*.

THEATRE
Kourion
Classical dramas are held throughout the summer months in the ancient open-air amphitheatre. An experience not to be missed. Ask the tourist office.

WEST
CULTURAL CENTRES
Paphos

Town Hall *28 Oct St (tel: 06 232804)*. Lectures in the evening.

CINEMAS
Paphos
Atheneum, *23 Kiazim Osman Pasha St (tel: 06 236934)*.

DISCOTHEQUES
Paphos
Boogies, *14 Ayios Antonios Street (tel: 06 244810)*.
Eros Disco, *1 Ayios Anastasias Street (tel: 06 234635)*.
Rainbow Disco, *Ayias Antonios/Ayia Napas streets (tel: 06 245471)*.
Samba Disco, *1 Archimidous Street (tel: 06 235922)*.

NORTH
CASINOS
Famagusta
Palm Beach *(tel: 036 62001)*.
Salamis Bay *(tel: 036 67200)*.
Kyrenia
Dome Hotel *(tel: 081 52453)*.
Grand Rock Hotel *(tel: 081 52238)*.
Liman Hotel *(tel: 081 52001)*.
Celebrity Hotel, *14km west of town (tel: 082 18751)*. Roulette and blackjack.

CULTURAL CENTRES
Nicosia
Atatürk Cultural Centre. Seminars
British Council, *23 Mehmet Akif Avenue (tel: 020 74938)*. Exhibitions and video shows.
Famagusta
Liberty Stadium, *Akdogan.*

DISCOTHEQUES
Famagusta
Palm Beach Hotel *(tel: 036 62000)*.
Salamis Bay Hotel *(tel: 036 67200)*.
Kyrenia
Grand Rock Hotel *(tel: 081 52238)*.
Dome Hotel *(tel: 081 52453)*.
Mare y Monte Hotel, *11km west of the town (tel: 082 18310)*. Open-air, by the sea.

NIGHTSPOTS
Some restaurants with live bands encourage impromptu performances by customers.

PUBS AND BARS
Kyrenia
Lots by the harbour. The Limani is popular.

THEATRES
Nicosia
Cyprus-Turkish State Theatre.
Famagusta
Municiple Theatre.

Children

*T*he Cypriots love children and they are welcome everywhere. So far this love has not embraced the provision of facilities such as ice rinks, water parks and marine lands. Perhaps they are not important in a country where the sun shines 340 days in the year. Certainly they do not need to provide such facilities to attract visitors. So what are the children to do? Well they can try the following.

BEACH

There is no need here to extol the virtues of sea and sand in warm weather, but buckets and spades will go well with the younger children, and pedalos and canoes for the older.

FISHING

A cheap rod and line in the shallows can give hours of fun and perhaps the occasional bite.

HORSE RIDING

Beach donkeys never caught on but there are some horse riding centres dispersed about the island, with trekking in the Troodos Mountains (see Sports).

KITES

These are not all that common in Cyprus and go down rather well. Most beaches are a little too busy for adventurous flying. If on the cliff-top, it is essential to keep the kite airborne at all times, as retrieval through the spikey brush can be painful.

LUNA PARKS (FUN FAIRS)

If the Cypriots are making one concession to manufactured children's entertainment, then this is it. All the resorts have them, but probably Nicosia has the best. They vary from modest affairs, with a handful of fruit machines and star wars games, to patches of land given over to ingenious tilting machines and go-kart tracks. Here, complete with helmet, the youngsters can whizz round and round and be champion for half a day. The one at Ayia Napa by the harbour has a miniature dodgem rink.

PARKS

There are not many, but where they do exist swings and roundabouts are there for the taking.

REPTILE HOUSE

By the harbour in Limassol is a reptile house. It contains various native lizards and some more exotic creatures such as crocodiles.

ZOO

Cyprus has two zoos. The one at Limassol is modest and the one at Larnaca very modest. The variety of species is limited but they are the best in Cyprus.

Children playing on a beach

Sport

ANGLING

Thirteen dams in Cyprus have freshwater fishing possibilities throughout the year. Species are trout, carp, mosquito fish, perch, catfish, silver bream. Special licences are required, available from the district fisheries department in:

Nicosia *(tel: 02 403527)*,
Larnaca *(tel: 04 630294)*,
Limassol *(tel: 05 330470)*,
Paphos *(tel: 06 240268)*.

Dams
Nicosia district
Athalassa dam, Lymbia dam
South
Kalavassos dam, Lefkara dam, Polemidhia dam, Yermasoyia dam
West
Argaka Makounta dam, Asprokremmos dam, Ayia Marina dam, Mavrokolymbos dam, Pomos dam
Troodos
Kafizes dam, Lefka dam

Limited fishing is also possible in the following dams: Kalopanayiotis,

There are many more fish in the sea!

Palaichori, Prodromos, Xyliatos. Amateur anglers are welcome to fish in the sea without a licence. There are, however, restrictions on the number of hooks and the species to be caught.

ATHLETICS TRACK AND FIELD

Although Cyprus is not at the forefront of world athletics, track and field events are popular and many Cypriots take a regular run or jog.

Nicosia
Makarion Athletics Centre, *Makedonitissa, 6km southeast from the city centre (tel: 02 350850)*. 400m tartan track, 8 lanes: 40m indoor track.
Larnaca
Zeno Athletics Centre, *3km west of city centre* . 400m clay track.
Zeno Stadium, *Artemis Avenue, in town centre (tel: 04 654927)*. Clay track.
Limassol
Tsirion Athletics Centre, *5km north of the town centre (tel: 05 333311)*. 400m tartan track, 8 lanes: 40m indoor track.
Paphos
Athletics Centre, *3km east of town centre*. 400m clay track.
Polis
Chrysochous Stadium

The Cyprus car rally is only for the brave!

BADMINTON

International events are staged from time to time.

Nicosia
Lefkotheo Sports Centre, *Makarion Athletics Centre, Makedonitissa, 6km south of the city centre (tel: 02 350270).*
Keravnos Athletic Club, *Strovolos, 3km southwest of city centre (tel: 02 313936).*
Larnaca
Municipal Sports Centre, *Phaneromeni Avenue centre of town.*

BASKETBALL

Nicosia
Lefkotheo Sports Centre, *Makarion Athletics Centre, Makedonitissa, 6km south of the city centre (tel: 02 350270).*
Keravnos Athletic Club, *Strovolos, southwest of city centre (tel: 02 313936).*
Pallouriotissa Sports Hall, *Pallouriotissa, east of city centre.*
Larnaca
Municipal Sports Centre, *Phaneromeni Ave, centre of town.*
Dherinia Sports Hall, 3km *north of Paralimni.*
Limassol
Olympia Sports Hall, *Tsirion Stadium, 5km northwest of city centre (tel: 05 387370).*
Athletiki Enosis Lemessou, Gladstone St *centre of town (tel: 05 362598).*

BOATING

Speed boats can be hired to roar up and down the coast. Alternatively one can join a group for a day's cruising.

BOWLING (TEN PIN)

Nicosia
Kykko Bowling, *near the Ledra Hotel, 5km southwest from the city centre (tel: 02 450085).*
Limassol
Limassol Bowling, *hotels area east of town centre (tel: 05 370414 and 370886).*

CYCLING

There are hundreds of bikes to be hired in all the resorts and many holidaymakers take to two wheels. Official literature suggests cyclists should keep off main roads at weekends because of the volume of traffic.
The **Cyprus Cycling Federation** *(tel: 02 450875)* organises competitions in spring and autumn. Anyone can take part.

CYPRUS CAR RALLY

This is held in September and attracts entries from many countries and includes championship drivers. Winding mountain roads and dirt tracks make it a tough proposition for car and driver.

Dhassoudi Beach, Limassol

DIVING

Spear fishing with aqualung requires a special licence. Certified divers can obtain this without trouble from the District Fisheries Departments (see **Angling** for telephone numbers). Decompression chambers exist at Nicosia and Akrotiri hospitals (see page 180 for telephone numbers).

It is forbidden to remove antiquities and sponges from the seabed.

Organised sub-aqua clubs and diving centres can be found in all the towns and resorts, as well as at a number of hotels. In addition various sporting shops sell or hire equipment.

FOOTBALL

Football at international level is played in Limassol's **Tsirion Stadium**. Local teams play in the Cyprus league. There are league grounds in **Nicosia, Larnaca, Ayia Napa, Paralimni, Dherinia, Limassol** and **Paphos**. In the north, football is played in the **Ruso Stadium**, Nicosia.

GYMNASTICS

Nicosia
Lefkotheo Sports Centre, *Makarion Athletics Centre, Makedonitissa, 6km south of the city centre (tel: 02 350270).*
Limassol
Olympia Sports Club, *Tsirion Stadium, 5km northwest of the city centre (tel: 05 333311).*

HANDBALL
Same venues as basketball, but not at Athletiki Enosis Lemessou.

HANG GLIDING
This is being promoted in north Cyprus by the **North Cyprus Turkish Aviation Association** *(Nicosia Airport, tel 02 314724)*. The Kyrenia Hills would seem ideal.

HORSE RACING
This is confined to Nicosia in the Greek sector. Race meetings on the flat take place at weekends and occasionally mid-week. The course is near St Paul's Street, Ayios Dhometios, west of the city.

HORSE RIDING
Nicosia
Lapatsa Sports Centre, *near Pano Dheftera, 11km southwest of Nicosia (tel: 02 621201)*. Incorporates a horse riding school for beginners up to advanced level.
Limassol
Elias Beach Horse Riding Centre, *8km east of the hotels of Limassol (tel: 05 325000)*. Open all the year round (closed midday).
Paphos
Paphos Riding Centre, *Tombs of the Kings area*. Open all year round.

Horses and ponies can be hired for trekking through the Troodos Hills.

JUDO/KARATE
As basketball.

MOTOR CYCLING
The bikes vary from the moped type to the fairly powerful. They are very popular, obvious dangers not withstanding. Some are eminently suitable for exploring the various tracks where motor cars would be ill advised to go. They can be hired in most towns.

SAILING
Larnaca
Larnaca Marina has berthing facilities for 350 yachts *(tel: 041 53110)*.
Limassol
Sheraton Pleasure Harbour is found by the hotel, east of Limassol. It has berths for 227 craft *(tel: 051 21100 ext 3312)*.

There are nautical clubs at Limassol, Larnaca, Paphos and Kyrenia as well as inland Nicosia

Less ambitious sailing, although perhaps nearly as much fun, can be had by hiring dinghies off any of the beach resorts.

SHOOTING
Hunting is controlled. Hares and partridges can only be shot between October and January, and woodpigeon can be shot between June and September. There are several clubs throughout the island.

Nicosia Shooting Club, *Yeri, 8km southeast of the city centre (tel: 02 482660)*. Open: weekends only.
Larnaca Shooting Club, *Kamares, 4km northwest of city centre (tel: 04 654378)*. Open: Wednesday, Saturday and Sunday.
Famagusta District Shooting Club, *Paralimni* (tel: 03 821418). Open: Wednesday, Saturday and Sunday.
Limassol Shooting Club, *Polemidia, 8km northwest of the city centre (tel: 05 363613)*. Open: Wednesday, Saturday and Sunday.
Paphos Shooting Club, *Anatoliko, 12km east of Paphos (tel: 06 232081)*. Open: Wednesday, Saturday and Sunday.

Boats at Larnaca marina

SKIING

Yes, it is possible to ski in Cyprus! But only just, for Mount Olympus, at 1,950m above sea-level, is the only peak that catches snow. There are four short runs of about 200m in length in Sun Valley. Over on the north face there are five more-demanding descents, of twice the length. Good skiers, however, will not find them difficult. For cross-country skiers there are, in theory at least, two tracks 4km and 8km long.

Ski equipment and sledges can be hired at the cabin in Sun Valley 1.

At weekends it is as well to get to the slopes early if equipment is wanted. If peace and quiet is desired then go mid-week.

Competitions are held from time to time at weekends on the north face.

The season runs from the first week in January to the end of March and sometimes longer. Vast amounts of snow falls regularly and melts fairly rapidly when the sun comes out. Nevertheless, proper clothing is a necessity. Powder snow is quite rare.

The slopes can be reached in about an hour from Nicosia and Limassol. Early arrivals might well beat the snow plough and find the last 800m

Ski club near Troodos

impassable without wheel chains.

For anyone wishing to stay overnight, Troodos has two hotels and Platres several. Neither place caters for apres-ski, but the best hope is Platres.

Ski Federation in Nicosia, *P O Box 2185, Nicosia (tel: 02 365340 during working hours, otherwise 02 456433).*

SQUASH

Nicosia
Eleon Sports Centre, *3 Ploutarchos Street, Engomi, southwest of city centre (tel: 02 449923).*
Lapatsa Sports Centre *(tel: 02 621201).*
Pano Dheftera, *16km southwest of Nicosia*
Lyra Sport Center, *Gr Digensis Ave, near Ledra Hotel (tel: 02 351200).*

SWIMMING
Sea

The clear blue Mediterranean waters and long stretches of sandy beach provide excellent opportunities for swimmers and bathers alike. On every beach, red buoys indicate the swimming areas. Three Cyprus Tourism Organisation (CTO) public beaches, all in attractive sites, offer full facilities to swimmers, including changing rooms and beach furniture for hire, as well as beachside refreshment areas. CTO Tourist Assistants supervise these beaches and lifeguards are usually present.

Pools
Nicosia
Olympic Pool, *5 minutes drive from the city centre, in the Goal area.* Leisure and diving pools (heated).
Eleon Pool, *3 Ploutarchos Street, Engomi, southwest of city centre (tel: 02 449923).* Day members welcome. Open- air, but closed in winter.
Limassol
Heated pool, *Dassoudi Tourist Beach, hotels area.*
Larnaca and **Paphos** have 25m heated pools.

TENNIS

Many of the big hotels have tennis

Bearded palms on seafront at Larnaca

courts which are not generally open to the public. The following centres are open to the public:

Nicosia
Eleon Tennis Club, *3 Ploutarchos Street, Engomi, southwest of the city centre (tel: 02 449923).*
Field Club, *Egypt Avenue, centre of town (tel: 02 452041).*
Lapatsa Sports Centre, *Pano Dheftera, 16km west of Nicosia (tel: 02 621201).*
Limassol
Limassol Sports Club, *11 Olympian Street, to the west of the town centre (tel: 05 359818).*
Larnaca
Larnaca Tennis Club, *Kilkis Street, in the town centre (tel: 041 56999).*
Paphos
Yeroskipos Tourist Beach, *2.4km east of Paphos (tel: 06 234525).*

VOLLEYBALL
As basketball.

WALKING
Around the resorts some effort has been made to accommodate strollers by constructing pavements between likely destinations.

In the hills nature trails are being blazed everywhere. Perspiring ramblers are educated at regular intervals with details of all the flora, in Greek and Latin. The start of a walk is usually marked with a gate: in effect, a small pitched roof on two posts. The Tourist Office claims four such trails in Troodos and will issue sketch maps and details on request. In fact, there are many more on the island, with several near the Baths of Aphrodite in the Akamas, and others in the Paphos Forest and above Khandria in central Troodos. Midsummer is far too hot for walking; even the mountain temperatures are too much for most people.

Walkers should take plenty of water with them. Big heavy boots are not necessary in the dry season, comfortable trainers with a good sole being perfectly adequate. In winter, the mountains can be cold, wet and cloudy, and Mount Olympus can be almost arctic, so proper clothing and footwear are required and a compass would be useful. There are many good clear days when it will be warm in the sun. Large-scale maps are needed on many walks and the 1:50,000 scale British Ministry of Defence series, K717 are invaluable. Try the Department of Lands and Surveys in Nicosia (tel: 02 403390). In the northern hills walkers will have problems of access in some areas because of military camps.

WATER SKIING
Early morning and late afternoon provide the calmest water. There can be much waiting around for the boat, the driver, or the equipment. But once underway, all is forgiven. The runs down the east coast at Fig Tree Bay are marvellous.

WINDSURFING
All the main beaches have a selection of boards for hire. Courses of instruction are available, and beginners will waste their time and money if they try to go it alone. Experienced board sailors will be disappointed that strong winds are infrequent in summer.

Food and Drink

*O*wning a restaurant seems to be the main occupation of an enormous number of Cypriots. From small ramshackle tavernas to sophisticated cosmopolitan establishments, there are a multitude of places to eat. It is, of course, also the main occupation of Cypriots who have moved abroad. Service is usually attentive and efficient. There are a wide range of dishes available, both traditional Greek and international. The Cypriots make brave attempts at providing translations, but this can have entertaining results.

FOOD

DISHES

Soups
Avgolemono: chicken stock in egg and lemon.
Psarosoupa: fish and vegetable soup.

Dips
Taramosalata: smoked cods' roe.
Tahini: sesame-seed paste.
Houmous: chickpea puree.

Meat Dishes
Kotopoulo: chicken
Pork
Souvlakia (kebab): meat on skewers served with salad and pitta bread.
Afelia: pork marinated in red wine.
Lounza: smoked pork (like bacon) served grilled.
Beef
Stifado: Beef casserole in red wine.
Lamb
Tavas: lamb casserole.
Kleftiko: slow roasted lamb cooked in a traditional Kleftiko oven.

Other meat dishes
Moussaka: minced lamb with layers of potatoes, aubergines in bechamel sauce.
Sheftalia: a type of sausage often in pitta bread.

Kestefhedes: meatballs.
Kypriakes ravioles: ravioli stuffed with halloumi cheese.
Dolmades: stuffed vine leaves.

Fish
In good fish restaurants the fish is kept live, in a tank, and you can select the particular fish you want.
Barbounia: red mullet.
Xyphias: swordfish.
Kalimari: squid in rings.
Octopus: steamed in red wine.

Salads
Salads accompany most meals. The ingredients tend to depend on season but usually contain tomatoes, cucumber and fetta cheese. What is known as Greek salad in Greece tends to be known as village salad in Cyprus.

Cheese
Fetta: white cheese made from sheep's

A gastronomic delight

milk, usually found in Greek salad.
Halloumi: white cheese made from goat's
milk. This is very popular.

Sweets

Baklava: sweet pastry with cinnamon
and nuts.
Kadaiffi: a similar sweet with a funny
shredded wheat like casing.
Loukoumia: Cyprus Delight (Turkish
Delight).

Fruit

There is always a tempting selection of
fruit available in Cyprus; melon is often
served as a dessert.

Coffee

Coffee is served at the end of most
meals. There is a wide range of different
types from Nescafé to Greek coffee
(formerly Turkish coffee). It is served in
small cups in three strengths; medium,
sweet, or unsweetened.

Cake Shops

Tourists can sometimes miss these
establishments which have a huge range
of sweet cakes and biscuits wrapped to
take away or simply to be eaten on the
spot, accompanied by a glass of water.

A very similar range of food is available
in the Turkish side of the island. Some
Turkish Cypriot cooking is an interesting
combination of traditional methods and
modern scientific gastronomy. There are
delicious snack mezes and some good
fresh fish dishes. *Siskebap* is lamb
roasted on a skewer and served with rice.
Doner-kebab is lamb or beef roasted on a
turning skewer and then cut in thin
slices.

DRINK

A fine selection of wines is available on
the island which are becoming

increasingly popular.

One of the most well known wines is
Commandaria St John. It is a fortified
dessert wine, first produced in the
Middle Ages for the Knights of St John
at Kolossi. Much was exported and it
was apparently well appreciated by the
Plantagenet kings of England.

Most of the island's white wines are
dry. Some of the best-known are **Keo
Hock, White Lady, Aphrodite** and
Arsinoe, which is a wine of delicate
character, some specimens being of 1962
vintage. Two of the most popular red
wines are **Othello** and **Afames**. The
latter is dry and full-bodied, reminiscent
of Burgundy wines.

None of these wines are available in
the north where the wine industry is very
much in its infancy. **Kantara** white and
red are the most widely available.

Light beers are a very popular way of
quenching thirst on a hot day. The
locally made **Keo** and **Carlsberg** are on
offer everywhere in the south. Imported
beers and lagers are not as readily
obtainable and are more expensive.

Brandy is a common after-dinner
drink and also appears as brandy sour,
when it is mixed with lemon juice,
bitters and soda water. The strong
Adonis brandy is matured for about 15
years.

Ouzo is a powerful aniseed-flavoured
drink which is something of an acquired
taste and needs to be treated with
caution.

There is, of course, **Cyprus sherry**.
Lysander is offered in extra dry, pale,
medium and cream. Only selected white
grapes are used for these sherries. They
are matured for at least two years in
French oak pipes.

In the north, brandy, raki and
zivania are very popular.

Restaurants

Restaurant prices in Cyprus fall into a relatively narrow charge band. Humble establishments are very cheap, but even at the other end of the scale, the most exclusive of places cannot be said to be extravagantly expensive. One reason for this is perhaps the attitude of the Cypriots, who consider a difference in price of three or four pounds to be enormous. This does not necessarily explain the convergence of prices in the tourist centres, but competition is a factor. Also government regulations may contribute. At the begining of the season all café and restaurant owners must submit their menu charges to a regulating body. Once these are approved they can be lowered but not increased. This is a device to protect the tourist against over-charging. However, few restaurants dare to stand out with prices higher than the average. This also applies to the drinks.

It may seem ridiculous but if one partakes of all the courses on offer, the price in most restaurants seems to end up at about CY £6.50, although shared mezes, fish and lobster dishes do affect this hypothesis. On top of this, a large beer will be 60 to 80 cents, a bottle of local wine about CY £2.30. It is possible to eat at half this cost but nearly impossible at double. Foreign wines do, however, cost more than twice as much as the local bottles.

The following is an approximate comparison guide with the restaurants in Britain.

£ Cheap: will cost CY £3.50. This will be good local food in basic surroundings.

££ Average: is about CY £6.50.
£££ Top price: is about CY £12.00.

Visitors should choose an establishment frequented by locals, where the food will be better and cheaper, and the atmosphere a lot livelier and friendlier.

For those wanting something different and not just in the way of food, the walled city of Nicosia is *the* place. Famagusta Gate area has been developed by the locals for the locals. The restaurants are uniquely Greek and the surroundings and atmosphere extraordinary, being right on the Green Line. No concessions are made to tourists, although they are welcome in twos and threes. One such establishment is arranged around a small courtyard and is combined with an interesting bookshop. The proprietor refuses to be listed but is very happy to receive visitors who seek him out. The food is Greek and medium price. Care should be taken walking in this part of the city; perhaps it is the frustration of the military divide that makes the Cypriots drive so fast in these confined streets.

Restaurant menu boards

NICOSIA

Abu Faisal
Serves pure Lebanese food and is combined with an art gallery. *31 Klimentos Street (tel: 02 443763).* ££

Astakos
Fish restaurant. *6 Menelaos Street, Engomi (tel: 02 353700).* ££

Axiothea
Greek food in lovely old house. Chairs and tables in street. Use the Green Line as a back rest. *Axiothea Street (tel: 02 430787).* ££

Bastioni
Piano Bar with floor show. Light food among the beautiful people. *Famagusta Gate (tel: 02 433101).* ££

Chang's China Restaurant
Chinese food, lunch and dinner. Closed Sundays. *Acropolis-Parthenon Street, Engomi (tel: 02 351350).* ££

El Grecos
Byzantine cooking in olde Cyprus surroundings. Meze ends with a T-bone steak. Vegetarian menu. *3 Menandros Street (tel: 02 474566).* ££

Fytron
Vegetarian wholefood with organic vegetables. Open for lunch and takeways. Closed weekends. *11 Chytri St, by health food stores (tel: 02 461466).* ££

Hilton Hotel
Orangery: à la carte, family brunch on Sundays, business lunches. Fontana Amorosa: Coffee or full meal, Cypriot and international cuisine. *Makarios Avenue (tel: 02 464040).* £££

Navarino Wine Lodge
Buffet in wonderful garden in fine old building. *1 Navarinou Street (tel: 02 450775).* ££

Skorpios
Excellent à la carte French and Cypriot cuisine in fine surroundings with first-class service. Cocktail bar upstairs. *3 Stassinos Street, Engomi (tel: 02 445950).* £££

Trattoria Romantica
Italian restaurant and steakhouse. *13 Pallikarides Street (tel: 02 465276).* ££

VIP's
French cuisine, lunch and dinner. Closed Sundays. *15 Chiou Street, Ay. Omoloyitae (tel: 02 458448).* ££

SOUTH EAST

LARNACA TOWN
The seafront is one restaurant after another. There is not much to choose between them. None is exciting but most are satisfactory.

Customers at a Paphos restaurant

Dionyssos Steakhouse
Grills and steaks on the seafront. Closed Tuesdays. *7b Ankara Street (tel: 04 653658).* ££

Megalos Perfkos
Fish, Cyprus meze and steaks. *Athens Avenue, by the fort (tel: 04 628566).* ££

To Dichoro
Charcoal grill, steaks and Cypriot specialities. *Near south end of Zenon Kitieos Street.* ££

LARNACA DHEKALIA ROAD
The following restuarants are grouped together and serve the clientele of the large hotels on this stretch of coast as well as the British forces of the nearby Dhekalia base. They are to be found about 300m from the Palm Beach Hotel near the turning for Pyla. The Roast Inn is a little nearer Larnaca than the rest, the Sussex nearer Dhekalia.

Dragon III
Specialised Cantonese cooking with 133 different dishes. *(tel: 04 644220).* ££

French Rendez Vous
Quality French food including fondue. Closed Tuesday. ££

Manhattan
Family bar and restaurant. *Opposite Lordos Hotel (tel: 041 22281).* ££

Pyla Fish Restaurant
First-class food from experts in this field. *(tel: 04 644254).* ££

Roast Inn
Carvery and Sunday lunch. *(tel: 04 628966).* ££

Sussex
Grills, steaks, curry, and English Sunday lunch. *Near Golden Bay Hotel (tel: 04 622211).* £

AYIA NAPA
Clarabell
International and Cyprus cuisine with a variety of fish dishes. Has a pleasant roof garden. *Makarios Avenue.* ££

Dragon I
Cantonese cooking. *Makarios Avenue (tel: 03 721585).* ££
Napa Castle
Cypriot cuisine and a variety of steaks. *Ayia Napas Avenue, above monastery (tel: 03 721697).* ££
Vip's
International cuisine. *Makarios Avenue (tel: 03 721540).* ££

PROTARAS
Baita
Italian restaurant. *South end of inner link road, near Sunrise Hotel (tel: 03 831174).* ££
Dragon II
Peking duck and 102 different dishes. ££
El Malu
International cuisine, fresh fish. *South end of inner link road, near Sunrise Hotel (tel: 03 831316).* ££
Promises
Grills and steaks on a well designed first floor terrace. *South end of inner link road, near Sunrise Hotel.* ££
Protaras Restaurant
International cuisine. *(tel: 03 831466).* ££
Wellington Steakhouse
Steaks, fish, snails and children's menu. The lobster takes the price into the next category. *Matova, Pernera Area (tel: 03 831306).* ££

SOUTH

LIMASSOL
This city has hundreds of restaurants and the number is growing.

Assos
Famous for its meze, local dishes and salads. *Old Limassol–Nicosia Road, opposite Poseidonia Hotel (tel: 05 321945).* ££
Bella Italia
Pizzas and pastas. *Potamos Yermasoyia, 3.5km east of municipal gardens and zoo (tel: 05 311114).* ££
Fiesta
International cuisine and Italian pastas. Overlooking the sea. *Georgiou A Avenue, Potamos Yermasoyia, 4.5km east of municipal gardens and zoo.* ££
Mikri Maria
Unusual and exceedingly small restaurant in a backwater run by two Cypriot ladies. Some English spoken. *3 Akyras Street, near castle (tel: 05 357679).* £
Neo Phaliro
Greek food, a great favourite with the locals and few concessions to tourism. The fish courses will take it into the next price category. *Gladstone Street, Old Town (tel: 05 365768).* ££
Old Harbour (Ladas)
Big fresh fish on charcoal. Fine place and popular with the locals. *Old harbour (tel: 05 365760).* £££
Pan Ku
Chinese cuisine including chow mein, chicken curry, chop suey. *Potamos Yermasoyia, 3.5km east of the municipal gardens and zoo (tel: 05 322302).* ££
Yildizlar
Lebanese food. Closed Monday. *Old Limassol-Nicosia Road, near turning to Ayios Tykhonas (tel: 05 322755).* ££

WEST

CORAL BAY
Corallo
Excellent mixed grill and good in all respects. *Peyia (tel: 06 621052).* ££

PAPHOS
Esperides Garden Restaurant
Excellent Cypriot and international cooking. *28 Poseidonos Avenue, Kato Paphos (tel: 06 238932).* ££
Garfield's Steak and Seafood
St Antoniou Street (tel: 06 236526). ££
Golden Dragon
Chinese food. Closed Tuesday. *Ayios Antonios, Kato Paphos (tel: 06 242896).* ££

Gondola
Italian restaurant.
St Antoniou Street (tel: 06 244717). ££.
Kings
Fish meze, seafood grills, and steaks. *The harbour (tel: 06 232158). ££*
Phuket
Chinese cuisine. *Tombs of The Kings Road (tel: 06 236738). ££*
Raffles
International cuisine in good surroundings.
Tombs of the Kings Road (tel: 06 248819). ££
Taj Mahal
Indian and Persian dishes. *Tombs of the Kings Road (tel: 06 238639). ££*

POLIS
Chix-Chox
Local and international cuisine but served at slow Polis pace. *Central Square (tel: 06 321669). ££*

TROODOS

PLATRES
Lanterns Hotel
Good local and international food in chaotic surroundings. *(tel: 05 421434). £*

NORTH

NICOSIA
Anbial
Meze and kebab. *East end of Green Line, by Famagusta Gate (tel: 020 71835). ££*
Saray Roof
International and Turkish cuisine with excellent view over the city. *Ataturk Meydani (tel: 020 71115). ££*
Hanedan
International menu and good local cuisine but may close down soon. *6.5km west of city, on road to Guzelyurt. ££*

FAMAGUSTA
La Cheminee
French owners providing good French cuisine.
Outside the walled city, close to no man's land (tel: 020 664021). ££
Palm Beach Hotel
International and local menu *(tel: 036 62000). ££*

MAGOSA
Agora
Popular; earth-cooked kebabs. *17 Elmas Tabya Sokak (tel:65364). ££*

Food displays at Paphos hotel

SALAMIS
Eyva
Local food in unpretentious surroundings.
Salamis Road. ££
Salamis Bay Hotel
International fare *(tel: 036 67200). ££*

KYRENIA HARBOUR AREA
Halil's
Things are cooked Turkish style here. *Kordon Boyn Caddesi (tel: 081 52299). ££*
Harbour Club
French cuisine upstairs, meze and local food outside on the pavement *(tel: 081 52211). ££*
Marabou
Good steaks and international cooking *(tel: 081 52292). ££*
Ristorante Italiano
Seafood in lovely walled garden. *West end of harbour (tel: 081 56845). ££*
Niazi's
Known for its kebab and fine steaks. *Kordon Boyn Caddesi (tel 081 52160). ££*

EAST OF KYRENIA, BELLABAYIS
Abbey House Restaurant
Some of the finest continental cuisine, advance booking advisable. *Bellabayis (tel: 081 53460). £££*

TOWARDS LAPTA, 8KM WEST OF KYRENIA.
Altinkaya
Very popular fish restaurant *(tel: 082 18341). ££*

Hotel Tips

*H*otels in Cyprus are graded between 'one-star' and 'five-star'. There are also 'hotels without a star' and 'guest houses'. The Cyprus Tourism Organisation booklet listing all the hotels and prices is essential for the independent traveller.

Cyprus has had an ambitious hotel building programme running over several years. Modest two-star establishments and luxurious five-star places have gone up virtually side by side. It has taken a water shortage to curtail the construction effort. This proliferation of accommodation means, of course, that visitors have a wide choice and a better chance of getting what they want.

MODERN HOTELS

All were built in a tremendous hurry with a labour force that, until a few years ago, was occupied on the land. This means that the plumbing can be erratic, and other details not quite right. And, of course, the coloured render and stucco can cover up a multitude of sins. Balcony rails may also be too low for real safety and perhaps not strong enough. In some bungalow hotels, guests may have to carry their cases 200m or more.

Notwithsanding the above, it has to be said that overall they come out very well. They are spacious, well decorated and efficiently run.

Real problems only seem to arise after a few years, if maintenance is not kept up. A good example is the lifts. Put in eight years ago with the cheapest tender they may seem unreliable today but they all have safe internal doors .

Ayia Napa Beach

One of the many seafront hotels at Limassol

Hotels with the two-star rating and below seem most vulnerable to maintenance difficulties.

OLD HOTELS

These are something of a variable commodity. The traditional design may be to the liking of many travellers and if part of a package deal, the tour operator will doubtless have checked them out thoroughly.

The new towns do not have this type of hotel, but most of the hill resorts have nothing else. Some are very good although most are likely to be in need of maintenance. A cheap one-star hotel can be, but not always, somewhat unsatisfactory.

FACILITIES

These are of course provided in direct proportion to the star rating. The more stars, the bigger the pool, and deeper blue the water. A one-star hotel will have either no pool or an unsatisfactory one. Five-star hotels have extra dining rooms and lounges, coffee shops, various bars and beach 'bars', shops and boutiques. However, the cost matches the opulence.

Three stars and above guarantees some evening entertainment. Certainly a Greek night and possibly bouzouki music and ballroom dancing.

AVAILABILITY

Accommodation for the summer does get snapped up early in the year, but last-minute offers are often made. Reductions for late bookings, with the resort unspecified, save money but are not always satisfactory. For example, Limassol is very different from Paphos. Also, a swimming pool or lack of one can make or break a holiday.

Out of season, visitors can sometimes negotiate a good price on some apartments. The solo traveller may well get a whole apartment at less than a hotel bed and breakfast room.

RECEPTION

English is always spoken and the receptionists are courteous. Any problems are generally resolved quickly. Money and travellers cheques can be changed at the desk although the banks give a better rate. Telephone calls can be made from the rooms and are not normally unreasonably surcharged.

MEALS

These are normally 'international' in preparation and content, with Greek fare once a week, and a barbecue evening. Evening meals are often available to bed and breakfast guests at prices well below the local restaurants. This is often exceptional value.

Breakfasts can be variable. A three-star hotel may provide a continental and English breakfast, all with fresh fruit. A two-star will charge extra for the English breakfast. Its continental breakfast can be a sumptuous affair or a mere two slices of toast with tea or coffee.

RATES

Greek Cyprus

Prices are quoted in Cyprus pounds per room daily (CY £1 = 100 cents).

Rates are approved by the Cyprus Tourism Organisation and they are all-inclusive (i.e they include the cost of hotel services, the percentage covering staff (10 per cent), taxes, and air-conditioning charge where a central system is in operation).

Many hotels publish maximum and minimum rates which relate to the particular characteristics of the room (size, view, furnishing) and not to any particular period of the year.

The rates quoted are for bed and breakfast, for half board (room, breakfast, lunch or dinner) and for full board (room, breakfast and dinner). The amounts indicated (supplement per person) are to be added. Those additions apply only to board arrangements contracted in advance and do not indicate regular meal prices.

Extras

(a) No extra charge may be made for heating.
(b) The extra charge for the use of air conditioning where this is optional (units) and requested by the guest, is £2.00 (maximum) per unit per day.
(c) For room service an extra charge of up to 50c may be made.
(d) In case a double room has to be offered for single occupancy, the hotel-keeper may charge 80 per cent of the daily room rate (accommodation only).
(e) In the case of hotel or tourist apartments, each additional person to the normal bed capacity of the apartment is charged by 50 per cent of the daily bed rate of the apartment.

Discounts

Most hotels offer discounts during the low season, on the accommodation rate, which for seaside resorts is from 16 November to 15 March (excluding the period 20 December to 6 January).

Discount for children occupying the same room as their parents:
Under 1 year, by private arrangement.
From 1 to 5 years, 50 per cent discount, on the accommodation per person daily rate.
From 6 to 10 years, 25 per cent discount, on the accommodation per person daily rate.

In case of three persons occupying a double room, the hotelkeeper is obliged to allow a discount of 20 per cent for the third person on accommodation.

Terms of Stay

Full board and half board rates apply to two full days of stay and over, as from the time of arrival.

During the months of July and August, hill resort hotels may charge guests wishing to stay at the hotel half board rates as a minimum term of stay.

No reduction is allowed for meals not taken when guests are staying on half or full board terms.

A bed and breakfast charge may be

Pavlo Napa Hotel, at Ayia Napa

A typical large, modern, seaside hotel at Limassol

made to guests using hotel accommodation overnight, irrespective of whether breakfast is taken or not.

Guests staying overnight are entitled to use the room up to 12 noon the next day. If the guest uses the room after this time and up to 6pm, he is liable to pay half a day's stay. Use beyond 6pm obliges the guest to pay for a whole day.

Turkish Cyprus

Prices are quoted in Turkish lira. A 10 per cent service charge and a 2 per cent municipal tax are added to prices.

Hotels provide bed and breakfast, half board and full board.

Extras

For room service an extra charge may be made.

Discounts

Hotels may offer a discount of up to 15 per cent during April and October, and up to 30 per cent from 1 November to 31 March.

Discount for children occupying the same room as their parents: under 2 years free, from 3 to 6 years 50 per cent, and from 7 to 12 years 25 per cent.

Terms of stay

No reduction is made for breakfast or meals not taken. Guests staying for the night are entitled to use the room up to 2pm; if the guest uses the room after this time and up to 6pm he is liable to pay a half day's stay. Use beyond 6pm obliges the guest to pay for a whole day.

OTHER ACCOMMODATION
Village Houses

Cyprus is now catering for visitors who care more about the countryside than beaches. The project is gradually spreading. Aiming to put money directly into the villages, the houses maintain their original exteriors but are renovated within.

Practical Guide

Contents

Arriving
Camping
Children
Climate
Crime
Customs Regulations
Disabled Travellers
Driving
Electricity
Embassies and Consulates
Emergency Telephone Numbers
Entry into North Cyprus from the South
Etiquette
Health
Hitch Hiking
Insurance
Language
Lost Property
Maps
Measurements
Media
Money Matters
National Holidays
Opening Times
Organised Tours
Pharmacies
Photography
Places of Worship
Post Offices
Public Transport
Senior Citizens
Student and Youth Travel
Telephones
Time
Tipping
Toilets
Tourist Offices

ARRIVING

By Air

In the Greek-controlled part of the island there are two airports, Larnaca and Paphos. Larnaca in the east is 6km from the town. It was built rapidly in 1975 when the previous international airport in Nicosia was put under UN control. It has since been extended to cope with the increasing traffic. Paphos airport, built much later, is small with a very provincial aspect. It is 13km from the town.

Most nationals require only a passport; this broadly covers visitors from the United Kingdom, the Commonwealth, the countries of Western Europe and the United States.

Immigration formalities are attended to fairly promptly in Cyprus. The stamp in your passport allows a stay of three months. No vaccination or health certificates are required for visitors.

Both airports have all the usual facilities of duty free shops, cafés and restaurants, although at Paphos the shop and café are very small. At the time of printing, the lounge in Paphos does not have air conditioning; fans at high level merely circulate warm air in summer.

There are no buses or service taxis to the airports, but there are plenty of ordinary taxis. Those on package deals will be met by a representative of the company and taken by bus to their resort.

Flights to north Cyprus arrive at Ercan airport, 37km from Kyrenia and 48km from Famagusta. No airline flies direct; all have to stop in Turkey to comply with formalities. The airport is of

Cyprus Airways plane at Larnaca Airport

the same standard as Paphos. *If asked, the immigration officer will stamp a piece of paper rather than the passport. Stamps from the north will prevent future entry to southern Cyprus.* The Greek Cypriot government has declared all visitors to the north, with the exception of those passing through the checkpoint in Nicosia, as illegal immigrants.

By Boat
Passenger services connect Cyprus with Piraeus, Rhodes, Haifa, Ashdod and Port Said. Most sailings are from Limassol with a few from Larnaca. Regular services do not commence until the spring.

In north Cyprus, a ferry connects Kyrenia with Tasucu and Selifke in southern Turkey. From Famagusta there is a year-round passenger and car ferry service to Mersin in Turkey. As with Ercan airport, the immigration officer will forego the passport stamp if asked (see arriving by air above).

Departure
Those on charter flights will have been given a telephone number to confirm their return flight, usually two days before leaving. The number is usually that of a local travel agent and it can be very difficult to get through.

Charter flights are notorious for being delayed. Try to check before leaving the hotel if the flight is late. If your flight is delayed do not go through immigration control until you have to; the departure lounge can get unbearably hot and crowded and the no smoking notices are often ignored.

CAMPING
Camping is only permitted on approved sites licensed by the tourist office. At present there are six such sites in the south and the amenities provided include electricity, toilets and showers, food shop and café and washing facilities. Nevertheless, the above provision varies in standard from site to site. Fees are approximately CY £1.50 per day for a tent or caravan space plus CY £1 per person per day. Tents are available for hire at several sites.

Sites
Ayia Napa
The site is to the west of the town, near Nissi Beach (tel: 03 721946). It has a capacity for 150 tents and caravans. Open March to October.
Larnaca
Forest Beach Camping (tel: 04 622414). The site is 8km east of the town in a clump of eucalyptus trees. Try and pitch your tent out of earshot of the busy main road. There is space for approximately 78 tents and caravans. Open April to October.
Limassol
Governor's Beach (tel: 05 632300). The site is 20km east of Limassol. Take junction 16 off the Limassol–Nicosia road. It is a new site with very good facilities and a capacity for 247 tents and 111 caravans. Tents are also available for hire. Open April to October.

Polis

The campsite is on the beach, 10 minutes walk from the town (tel: 06 321526). The site is very popular in summer. It has places for 200 tents and caravans. Open March to November.

Troodos

The site is just off the main Nicosia–Troodos road, 1km before Troodos Square (tel: 05 421624). This is an elevated site, at 1,700m above sea-level, which means it is very cold at night. Spaces are allocated among the pine trees. Open May to October.

Paphos

Yeroskipos Zenon Gardens (tel: 06 242277). Campers will find the site 2.5km east of Paphos and east of the tourist beach. The capacity is for 95 tents and caravans right by the beach. Open March to October.

A few private sites near beach restaurants and run by the owners, are permitted. The facilities are usually somewhat limited.

In north Cyprus there is one camp site at Kyrenia (Riviera Mocamp) and another at Famagusta (Onur).

CHILDREN

Children are generally safe in Cyprus. Cases of child molesting are virtually unknown. Great care should be taken to prevent children getting badly sunburnt. The other main dangers are at archaeological sites where unguarded battlements and unprotected drops are common.

Nappies and baby food are found in all major supermarkets and pharmacies.

CLIMATE

Cyprus is the hottest and driest island in the Mediterranean. It starts getting hot in May and by July and August is more than 30°C (90°F) on the coast and approaching 38°C (100°F) inland.

There is no rain between June and September and very little in May and October. The climate in the mountains is quite different, however; much cooler at night even in summer. But during the day it is still relatively hot. The sea is warm from the end of May to October.

November to April sees the worst of the weather. The main rain falls from December to February and it can feel quite cold, not least because Cypriot houses are built to cope only with the summer heat. However, the hotels are usually properly heated. It also gets dark early. April is the height of the spring in Cyprus which transforms the country into a blaze of flowers. However, by late summer the landscape becomes very dry and dusty.

> **Weather Chart Conversion**
> 25.4mm = 1 inch
> °F = 1.8 × °C + 32

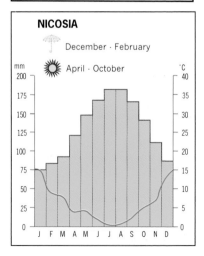

CRIME

There has been the occasional bag-snatching incident and murder, but really there is not much crime in Cyprus. Any problem in this respect is unlikely to be with the Cypriots, for they are generally honest and law abiding. The same cannot be said of all the tourists, therefore reasonable care should be taken over property. For example, the car should be locked, with belongings stored in the boot; money and jewellery ought to be kept in the hotel safe.

In the event of any incident the police should be contacted and are usually very helpful. Policemen are likely to speak English.

Many prices are set by the government and so it is easy to check whether you are being cheated. Hotel prices should be displayed on the room door; taxi prices in the vehicle.

CUSTOMS REGULATIONS

All travellers except transit passengers may bring into the island the following items free of duty:

Tobacco: 250grams
Spirits other than perfumed spirits: 1 litre
Wine: 0.75 litre (one bottle)
Perfume and toilet water: 0.30 litre, including one bottle of perfume of not more than 0.15 litre

Articles of any other description (except jewellery) up to a total value of the equivalent of CY £50. The above applies to the north and south.

However, when a passenger re-enters the Republic of Cyprus (southern Cyprus) after less than 72 hours he is allowed to import duty free only 250 grams of tobacco.

Currency controls exist and only CY £50 can be imported, or exported. Foreign exchange in excess of $1000 should be declared at customs on arrival so that there will be no problems on departure. (In reality it is unusual for anyone to be asked on departure what they are taking out.) There is no restriction on the amount of currency that can be taken into the north.

DISABLED TRAVELLERS

Disabled travellers need to prepare their trips carefully as there are very few facilities for them in Cyprus. The tourist office publish a leaflet which gives further information. Travel agents should also be able to give advice on the suitability of individual hotels.

Most villages and towns do not have complete pavements and there are few ramps. The main resorts are on fairly level ground with the exception of Ayia Napa and the upper town in Paphos.

DRIVING

Accidents

If you have an accident wait until a policeman arrives who speaks English. The Cypriots are very excitable in times of crisis, although their outrage may be tempered when encountering foreigners. It may be sensible to take a photograph of the scene. If not, take a sketch or drawing, with a note of any witnesses.

Breakdowns

Hire car companies issue a phone number to call in case of breakdown. Those travelling in the south with their own cars may be able to use the facilities of the **Cyprus Automobile Association** in Nicosia (tel: 02 313233).

Driving Standards

The roads are reasonable in Cyprus and British visitors have the distinct advantage of being able to drive on the left. They should be aware that Cypriots can be reckless drivers, with habits as bad as ignoring red lights and overtaking on bends.

Foreigners should take care at all times, particularly on mountain roads, and should make sure that their screen wash is topped up as roads get very dusty at the height summer.

Cars also get very hot if they are not parked in the shade. The steering wheel can be too hot to touch and it is worth using a car blind for the windscreen, or at least placing a towel over the steering wheel, and leaving the windows slightly open.

Finding your way

Finding your way is generally easy. Signposts are in English and Greek, and the main tourist sites marked with distinctive brown signs. Difficulties will be encountered in narrow village streets which have maze-like qualities and no signs. The best policy is to follow your instincts and the chances are you will emerge at the other side of the village,

Sign post in Greek and English

although it may take some time. If you are driving a large car it may be unwise even to attempt the narrower streets.

Motorists should beware of instructions given by locals. Directions drawn out with a stick in the dust should be treated with even more circumspection. Drivers should also beware of the statement 'the road is good'.

Visitors should be aware that there is a move under way to change some of the spellings of placenames. For example, Larnaca is becoming Larnaka and Khirokitia changes to Choirikitia while places named after saints are changing from ayia to agia. However, most of the changes are not significant enough to cause confusion.

Car Hire

There is an inordinate number of car hire companies in Cyprus, from the big international names to tiny local firms. Twenty-one is usually the minumum age limit and a national driving licence is required. There are four types of car, type A being the smallest and cheapest. Open-top jeeps seem to be the most popular vehicles.

Check what the price of hire includes, particularly for collison damage waiver without which visitors are repsonsible for up to £500 of any damage caused. Also scrutinise the state of the car, paying especial attention to tyres and brakes.

Very competitive rates are available to visitors who seek out the best prices and book in advance. It is much easier than hunting around in Cyprus.

In the north, car hire is much cheaper than in the south but the same principles apply. Most confusing is the fact that some firms hire out both left- and right-hand-drive cars despite the fact that driving in the north is on the left.

Insurance

If you bring your own car to Cyprus you must arrange specific cover for Cyprus. The green card is not valid.

Parking
Parking is generally easy. There are car parks in all the major towns, usually charging a small fee.

Petrol
There is a large number of petrol stations across the island, but most are shut on Sundays making it essential to fill up before the weekend.

Speed Limits
The speed limit on the new dual carriageways: 100kph.
Other rural roads: 80kph.
In towns: 50 kph.
Speed limits and distances in the south are in kilometres, in the north in miles. Front seat belts are compulsory.

ELECTRICITY
The electricity supply is 240 volts AC 50 cycles single-phase for lighting and domestic requirements. Socket outlets are for three-pin plugs. Adaptors are available in hotels and shops.
Apartments and hotels generally have a 110 volt outlet for shavers.

EMBASSIES AND CONSULATES
(As north Cyprus is not recognised by the international community these are all in the south)

Australian High Commission,
4 Annis Komninis Street, 2nd Floor, Corner Stassinos Avenue, Nicosia (tel: 02 473001).
British High Commission, Alexander Pallis Street, Nicosia (tel: 02 473131).
Canadian High Commission,
4 Queen Frederica Street, Suite 101, Nicosia (tel: 02 459830).
US Embassy, Dositheos and Therissos Street, Lycavitos, Nicosia (tel: 02 465151).

EMERGENCY TELEPHONE NUMBERS
South
In case of emergency, immediate response will be given by telephoning the following numbers. Emergency operators speak English.

Ambulance: 199 (all towns)
Fire Service: 199 (all towns)
Police: 199 (all towns)
Night Pharmacies: 192 (all towns)
General Hospitals:
Nicosia 02 451111
Limassol 05 330333
Larnaca 04 630311
Paphos 06 232364
Paralimni 03 821211
Polis 06 321431
Kyperounta 05 532021
Thomas Cook travellers Cheque loss or theft: 00 44 733 502995 (UK no, reverse charges). The local Thomas Cook offices listed on page 187 can offer emergency assistance.

North
Police:
Nicosia 020 83411
Kyrenia 081 52014
Famagusta 036 65310
First Aid:
Nicosia 020 71441
Kyrenia 081 52266
Famagusta 036 62876

ENTRY INTO NORTH CYPRUS FROM THE SOUTH
There is only one point of access along the entire 137km division. This is at the old Ledra Palace Hotel in Nicosia, on the west side of the walled city. This once-famous building is now sandbagged and in the control of the United Nations.
  The journey across the 'Green Line'

is from the south only and is for one day at a time. Visitors must return by 5.30pm and cannot cross the border into the north after 2pm. Passports are required and the procedure is to obtain clearance from the police at the Greek checkpoint, who record your passport number. Then walk through to the Turkish side. Here there is some form filling to complete and payment of CY £1.

People wishing to go further afield than Nicosia can hire a taxi to go to Kyrenia and/or Famagusta (or other places). They are not unduly expensive. Alternatively they can opt for a bus or hire a car. The Turkish Cypriot authorities, if asked, may say that the latter is not possible without notice, so it is best to try the hire companies direct. It may also be suggested that some tourist sites are not accessible, even though people already in the north visit them freely. Hired cars are not allowed through the control point. Most buses leave from Girne Gate.

It should also be realised that the border has, on occasions, been closed. For example, during the summer of 1988 nobody was allowed through for weeks on end. Current regulations therefore may change.

ETIQUETTE

In order to enter monasteries shoulders and legs need to be covered up (ie no shorts or backless dresses).

HEALTH

There are no inoculation requirements and no health certificates are needed.

The cost of medical facilities must be paid for, and visitors are strongly advised to take out holiday insurance.

General hospitals have casualty

departments for emergency cases. Hotels will make arrangements for medical services for their guests upon request.

Private doctors surgery hours (weekdays) 9am–1pm and 4pm–7pm.

Cyprus has a healthy climate and the water is safe to drink. However, it is good practice to wash all fruit.

Sunburn can be a problem. Even one hour in the sun on the first day will be enough to cause the fair skinned to burn.

Mosquitoes, although not malarial, are sometimes a nuisance. If the room is air conditioned, kill them before going to bed and keep the windows closed. Where windows have to be open, then a mosquito coil may help. Insect repellent should also be used.

There are at least two types of venomous snake in Cyprus. One is the viper, identified by its distinctive zigzag markings. It is unlikely to be encountered, but walkers and climbers in the hills, especially the Kyrenia range, need to keep a watch out. If bitten seek medical attention immediately. A serum is available on order from pharmacies for those who feel confident enough to use it.

HITCH HIKING

Hitch hiking is allowed and is generally safe, although single women should take care, especially in outlying areas at night. Visitors are most likely to be approached for lifts by young soldiers trying to return home on leave from their military service.

INSURANCE

Some form of holiday insurance is recommended. The important priority is to ensure that it covers medical expenses.

Driving insurance is included in the price of car hire. Check that it includes a collision damage waiver. Car insurance will not cover the underside of the car, so care is needed on bad roads. Drivers with their own cars will have to arrange cover specific to Cyprus. The green card is not valid.

LANGUAGE

Cyprus has always had two official languages, Greek and Turkish. The present division of the island means that Greek is spoken in the south and Turkish in the north. There is no need for English speakers to learn Greek, for many Greek Cypriots, including all those in the tourist industry, speak good English. An attempt at the language is useful in the village coffee shop and similar places, for here it will most likely lead to further conversation and the locals may know little or no English.

South

Alpha	Αα	nu	Νν
Beta	Βϐ	Xi	Ξξ
Gamma	Γγ	Omicron	Οο
Delta	Δδ	Pi	Ππ
Epsilon	Εε	Rho	Ρρ
Zeta	Ζζ	Sigma	Σσς
Eta	Ηη	Tau	Ττ
Theta	Θθ	Upsilon	Υυ
Iota	Ιι	Phi	Φφ
Kappa	Κκ	Chi	Χχ
Lambda	Λλ	Psi	Ψψ
Mu	Μμ	Omega	Ωω

Useful Words and Phrases
yes né
no óhi
please parakaló
thank you efcharistó
hello yásou
goodbye chérete
good morning kaliméra
good afternoon kalispéra

good night kaliníkta
today simera
tomorrow avrio
yesterday hthes
Sunday kiriaki
Monday theftera
Tuesday triti
Wednesday tetarti
Thursday pempti
Friday paraskevi
Saturday savaton
Bank trapeza
Bus leoforio
Car aftokinito
Where is...? pou iné?
How much? póso káni?
Do you speak English? milate angliká?
A room domatio

Numbers:

1	ena	9	ennia
2	thio	10	teka
3	tria	20	ikosi
4	téssera	100	ekató
5	pénte	200	thiakosi
6	éxi	500	pentakosi
7	eptá	1,000	chília
8	októ		

North

In the north, less English is spoken. Waiters often have only a limited fluency and some knowledge of Turkish is a definite advantage.

Signs have Turkish names for places better known by their Greek names, and maps are not always consistent. It is wise to have a map showing Turkish names.

Turkish	Greek
Girne	Kyrenia
Gazimagusa	Famagusta
Guzelyurt	Morphou
Lefkosa	Nicosia
Lapta	Lapithos
Besparmak	Pentadaktylos

The Turkish alpahabet is very similar to the Latin script with a few exceptions:

c = j in Jam
c = ch
s´ = sh
u = u as in French tu
i = a as in serial

Useful Words and Phrases

yes   evet
no   hayir
hello   merhaba
goodbye   allahaismarladik
good morning   gunyadin
good evening   iyi aksamlar
good night   iyi geceler
today bugun
tomorrow   yarin
yesterday dun
please   lutfen
thank you   mersi
Sunday   Pazar
Monday   Pazartesi
Tuesday   Sali
Wednesday   Carsamba
Thursday   Persembe
Friday   Cuma
Saturday   Cumartesi

Numbers:

1	bir	**30**	otuz
2	iki	**40**	kirk
3	uc	**50**	elli
4	dort	**60**	altmis
5	bes	**70**	yetmis
6	alti	**80**	seksen
7	yedi	**90**	doksan
8	sekiz	**100**	yuz
9	dokuz	**200**	iki yuz
10	on	**300**	uc yuz
11	on bir	**1,000**	bin
20	yirmi	**2,000**	iki bin

LOST PROPERTY

The Cypriots are honest people, and lost items may be quickly returned to their owners. Failing that, the local police station should be contacted. The loss of insured items and travellers cheques should also be immediately reported to the responsible authority listed in the documentation, assuming that it has not been lost as well.

MAPS

Except for Nicosia, there are free town maps available from the tourist offices together with a basic road map. A more detailed map may be useful for those intending to do a lot of driving on the island.

MEASUREMENTS

Cyprus uses metric weights and measures. Clothes and shoes use standard European sizes.

Conversion Table

FROM	TO	MULTIPLY BY
Inches	Centimetres	2.54
Centimetres	Inches	0.3937
Feet	Metres	0.3048
Metres	Feet	3.2810
Yards	Metres	0.9144
Metres	Yards	1.0940
Miles	Kilometres	1.6090
Kilometres	Miles	0.6214
Acres	Hectares	0.4047
Hectares	Acres	2.4710
Gallons	Litres	4.5460
Litres	Gallons	0.2200
Ounces	Grams	28.35
Grams	Ounces	0.0353
Pounds	Grams	453.6
Grams	Pounds	0.0022
Pounds	Kilograms	0.4536
Kilograms	Pounds	2.205
Tons	Tonnes	1.0160
Tonnes	Tons	0.9842

Men's Suits

UK		36	38	40	42	44	46 48
Rest of Europe	46	48	50	52	54	56	58
US		36	38	40	42	44	46 48

Dress Sizes

UK		8	10	12	14	16 18
France		36	38	40	42	44 46
Italy		38	40	42	44	46 48
Rest of Europe		34	36	38	40	42 44
US		6	8	10	12	14 16

Men's Shirts

UK	14	14.5	15	15.5	16	16.5	17
Rest of Europe	36		37	38	39/40	41	42 43
US	14	14.5	15	15.5	16	16.5	17

Men's Shoes

UK		7	7.5	8.5	9.5	10.5 11
Rest of Europe	41		42	43	44	45 46
US		8	8.5	9.5	10.5	11.5 12

Women's Shoes

UK	4.5		5	5.5	6	6.5	7
Rest of Europe	38	38	39	39	40	41
US		6	6.5	7	7.5	8	8.5

MEDIA

Greek Cyprus has an incredible 11 daily newspapers plus three weekly ones. The daily *Cyprus Mail* is in English as is the *Cyprus Weekly*. English and other European newspapers are on sale one day late. In the Turkish part of Cyprus they have the *Cyprus Times* in English.

Two radio channels are transmitted from the south, Channel 1 (VHF/FM 97.2MHz) is in Greek, Channel 2 (603KHz/498m and VHF/FM 94.8MHz) transmits programmes in English, Turkish, Armenian and Arabic. The latter gives news bulletins, weather forecasts followed by classical and popular music. From June to September a tourist programme called Welcome To Cyprus is broadcast on all days except Sunday. This is in five languages and covers such things as exchange rates, a comprehensive weather forecast and information on what to see and do. The English programme starts at 8.30am.

BFBS is the British Forces Broadcasting Service and it is on the air for 24 hours. The programmes are aimed at the forces personnel and cover many interesting matters as well as news. Northern Cyprus can tune into all the above stations.

Television programmes transmitted from the south are broadcast every evening and run from 5pm to 11pm in winter and 6pm to 11pm in summer. The entertainment is in colour and includes material from Britain and America, using the original language and Greek sub-titles.

Cyprus television is linked with Eurovision for live transmission of major athletic and other events.

MONEY MATTERS
Southern Cyprus

Greek Cypriot currency is the Cyprus pound which is divided into 100 cents. There are notes to the value of CY £10, CY £5, CY £1 and 50 cents. Coins are in demoninations of 1, 2, 5, 10 and 20 cents.

See also customs regulations.

Banks

Banks are open Monday to Friday 8.15am–12.30pm; Saturday morning opening has recently been withdrawn. However, in all the popular areas there are many banks offering afternoon tourist services. They are open to

Coins and notes

exchange money from 3.30pm to 5.30pm; sometimes to 7pm. Bank clerks speak good English.

Many hotels have exchange facilities but charge much higher commission than the banks.

A total of 4,000 shops, restaurants and hotels accept major credit cards; these are mainly in the tourist resorts. Money can also be withdrawn from the principal banks, and there are an increasing number of automatic cash dispensers which take credit cards. Thomas Cook travellers cheques in sterling are accepted by most hotels and many restaurants and shops in lieu of cash.

Northern Cyprus

Northern Cyprus uses the Turkish lira (TL). Notes go up to a value of 100,000 lira; coins cover values of 50, 100, 500 and 1,000 lira.

Banks

Banks in are open from 8am to 12 noon, Monday to Saturday; October to April from 8.30am-12 noon.

Credit cards are not widely accepted.

NATIONAL HOLIDAYS

All public services, private enterprises and shops are officially closed on National Holidays. In resort and coastal areas, however, shops and certain services remain open.

Southern Cyprus

1 January	New Year's Day
6 January	Epiphany Day
Variable	Green Monday (50 days before Greek Orthodox Easter)
25 March	Greek National Day
1 April	Greek Cypriot National Day
Variable	Good Friday (Greek Orthodox Church)
Variable	Easter Sunday
Variable	Easter Monday (Greek Orthodox Church)
1 May	Labour Day
Variable	Kataklysmos (Festival of the Flood)
15 August	Dormition of the Virgin Mary
1 October	Cyprus Independence Day
28 October	Greek National Day (Ohi Day)
25 December	Christmas Day
26 December	Boxing Day

Northern Cyprus

23 April	Children's Festival
19 May	Youth Festival
29 October	Turkish National Day
15 November	Turkish Cypriot National Day

The main Muslim holidays, Bayram at the end of the Ramadan Fast and the four-day Kurban Bayram (Birthday of the Prophet), move through the calendar.

OPENING TIMES
South
Shops and businesses
Summer (1 May–30 September):
Monday, Tuesday, Thursday, Friday
8am–1pm and 4pm–7pm. Wednesday
and Saturday half day closing,
8am–1pm.
Winter (1 October–30 April): Monday,
Tuesday, Thursday, Friday 8am–1pm
and 2.30pm–5.30pm. Wednesday and
Saturday, half day closing 8am–1pm.

Public Services
Summer (1 June to 30 September):
Monday to Saturday 7.30am–1.30pm.
Winter (1 October to 31 May):
Monday to Friday 7.30am–2pm and
Saturday 7.30am–1pm.

Museums and archaeological sites
These each have their own opening
times, see individual entries.

North
Shops
Summer: 7.30am–1pm and 4pm–6pm.
Winter: 8am–1pm and 2pm–6pm.
Early closing Saturday and closed all day
Sunday. Opening all day is becoming
fairly common.

Business Hours
Summer: 7.30am–1pm and
4pm–6.30pm, Monday to Friday, and
7.30am–1pm Saturday.
Winter: 8am–5pm Monday to Friday,
and Saturday 8am–1pm.

Public Services
Summer: 7.30am–2pm.
Winter: 8am–1pm and 2pm–5pm.

Museums and archaeological sites
These each have their own opening
times, see individual entries.

ORGANISED TOURS
Those on package deals will have plenty
of tours organised for them. These will
usually be by bus but although a good
way of getting away from the resorts they
may be too inflexible for the
independently minded.

There are boat trips from Paphos to
Lara; from Lachi to the Akamas
Peninsula; and trips from Ayia Napa to
Cape Greco. Hiking and jeep excursions
to the hinterland are organised by Exalt
Travel, PO Box 337, Paphos (tel: 061
43803).

For specific details, contact hotel
reception or the tourist office who have a
list of approved tour operators, or the
offices of the local Thomas Cook Network
Member, Huu Blym Araouzos, at:
143E Chr Hadjipavlou Street, Limassol.
67/68 Athens Street, Larnaca
17 Evagoras Avenue, Nicosia

PHARMACIES
Pharmacies are open during normal
shopping hours. The names of the duty
pharmacists are listed in the newspaper
or can be obtained by phoning 192.

All standard medicines and toiletries
are readily available. Not all drugs
require prescriptions.

PHOTOGRAPHY
In southern Cyprus there are many
photography shops selling all the well-
known brands of film and offering good
quality developing services. The largest
outlets are usually reliable.

There are restricted areas near
military camps and the border where
photography is forbidden.

Flash photography is not permitted inside churches.

Visitors to northern Cyprus should take their own film and batteries with them.

PLACES OF WORSHIP

The religion of southern Cyprus is Greek Orthodox. There are services every Saturday evening and Sunday morning. There are Anglican and Catholic churches in Nicosia, Limassol, Paphos and Larnaca.

Anglican churches

Nicosia: St Paul's, 2 Gr. Afxentiou Street.
Limassol: St Barnabas, 177 Leondios Street.
Paphos: Chrysopolitissa Church, Kato Paphos.
Larnaca: St Helena's, St Helena Building, flat 201.

Roman Catholic churches

Nicosia: Roman Catholic Church (Holy Cross), Paphos Gate.
Limassol: St Catherine's, 2 Jerusalem Street.
Paphos: Chrysopolitissa Church, Kato Paphos.
Larnaca: Terra Santa Church, Terra Santa Street.

There are mosques in all the main towns in northern Cyprus (see **What to See** section).

POLICE

Cypriot police are usually helpful and most speak English. There are also tourist office assistants in the resorts who will help visitors in trouble. The general emergency number is 199.

POST OFFICES
South

Open: 1 June to 30 September 7.30am–1pm, Monday to Saturday; 1 October to 31 May 7.30am–1.30pm.

Airmail letters take three to four days to reach Europe. Some shops and kiosks also sell stamps.

Every letter and postcard also has to have a 1 cent refugee stamp.

Main Post Offices (with poste restante services)
Nicosia: Eleftheria Square (tel: 02 303219).
Limassol: 1 Gladstone Street (tel: 05 330143/330114).
Larnaca: King Paul Square (tel: 04 652205).
Paphos: Themidos and St Paul Street (tel: 06 232241).

North

Open: 8am–1pm and 2pm–5pm, Monday to Friday; Saturday 8.30am–12.30pm.

All post from northern Cyprus goes via Turkey.

PUBLIC TRANSPORT
South

Buses

Inter-city and village buses operate between the main towns. Village buses tend to serve the needs of the local population, coming into town early in the morning and returning early afternoon.

There are regular services between the main towns until about 7pm. There are also frequent services between out-of-town hotels and the town centres or the beach. Information should be available at the hotels.

Main bus stations
Nicosia: Dionysos Square, west of Eleftheria Square on the walls (tel: 02 473414).
Larnaca: Hermes Street.
Limassol: Between the market and Anexartisias Street (tel: 05 370592).
Paphos: Pervola bus station, Thermopylon Street.

Taxis
Service taxis (shared taxis) operate between the main towns, usually every half hour. There are no service taxis to the airport or on Sundays. Seats can be booked in advance.

Rural taxis are available in the mountain villages.

Urban taxis are available in the main towns and serving the aiports. Fares are higher after midnight and there is an extra charge for luggage.

North
There are taxis, as in the south, offering both individual services and shared taxi routes. There are buses between the main towns, but information about their services can be hard to obtain.

SENIOR CITIZENS
Few concessions are made to the needs of the elderly visitor or the disabled. Most of the villages and many parts of the towns lack a complete pavement. Hotels do not have ramps; steps are everywhere.

SPORT
See page 160.

STUDENT AND YOUTH TRAVEL
Cyprus is not on the backpacker's route. There is no such thing as a really cheap air fare and budget accommodation is fairly limited. There are some campsites (see page 177) and the following is a list of *youth hostels:*
Nicosia: 13, Prince Charles Street, opposite Asty Hotel (tel: 02 444808). Open 7.30am–10am and 4pm–11pm.
Limassol: 120 Ankara Street, behind Limassol Castle (tel: 05 363749). Open 7.30am–11pm.
Larnaca: 27 Nicolaou Rossou Street, near St Lazarus Church (tel: c/o 04 621508). Open all year.
Paphos: 37 Eleftherios Venizelos Avenue (tel: 06 232588). Open 7.30am–10.30am and 4pm–10pm.
Troodos: 400m from Troodos Square on Kakopetria to Troodos road (tel: 05 421649). Open 7.30am–10.30am and 4pm–10pm, July and August only.
Stavros tis Psokas Rest House, Paphos Forest (tel: 06 722338 advance reservation essential).

TELEPHONES
Cyprus has a good telephone system with coin- and card-operated call boxes. Some phones in Polis have been vandalised and all towns have ones that frustratingly take only emergency 199 calls.Telephone enquiries: dial 192.

Instructions in the south are displayed in Greek and English. Coins accepted are 2, 10 and 20 cents. There is an increasing number of card phones taking cards to the value of £2 and £5, which are available from kiosks, post offices and banks.

International Codes
United Kingdom: 0044
US and Canada: 001
Australia: 0061

Telephone boxes

Local Codes
South
Nicosia: 02
Limassol: 05
Larnaca: 04
Paphos: 06
Ayia Napa and Protaras: 03
Platres: 05
Polis: 06

North
Nicosia (Lefkosa): 020
Kyrenia (Girne): 081
Famagusta (Gazimagusa): 036

TIME
Cyprus is two hours ahead of GMT; in summer clocks go forward one hour.

TIPPING
A 10 per cent service charge is included in hotel and restaurant bills. Porters and hairdressers appreciate a small tip, as do taxi drivers in the south. In the north it is not usual to tip taxi drivers.

TOILETS
There are public toilets virtually everywhere in the south but very few in the north. They are generally clean, or at least start out that way. By the end of the day they may be a little less than spotless. None have toilet paper. Toilet paper should not be put down the toilet but left in the bin provided.

TOURIST OFFICES
South
Main office (postal enquiries only): 18, Theodotou Street, Nicosia, PO Box 4535.
Nicosia: Laiki Yitonia (tel: 02 444264).
Limassol: 15 Spyros Araouzos Street (tel: 05 362756), or 35 George A Street, opposite tourist beach (tel: 05 323211).
Ayia Napa: 17 Arch Makarios Avenue (tel: 03 721796).
Larnaca: Democratias Square (tel: 04 654322).
Paphos: 3 Gladstone Street (tel: 06 232841).
Platres: (tel: 05 421316).

North
Nicosia (Lefkosa): (tel: 020 75051).
Kyrenia (Girne): harbour (tel: 081 52145).
Famagusta (Gazimagusa): (tel: 036 62864).

There are also tourist offices at the airports.

The tourist offices are open every morning except Sunday and on Monday and Thursday afternoons (see p186).

Offices Abroad
UK Cyprus Tourist Office, 213 Regent Street, London W1R 8DA (tel: 071 734 9822).
UK North Cyprus Tourist Office, 28 Cockspur Street, London SW1Y 5BN (tel: 071 930 4853).
US Cyprus Trade Centre, 13 East 40th Street, New York 10016 (tel: 212 2139100).
High Commission of the Republic of Cyprus, 37 Endeavour Street, Red Hill, ACT 2603 Canberra (tel: 62 952120).

A
accommodation
 hotels 172–5
 rented rooms 14
 village houses 175
 youth hostels 189
airports and air services 176
Akamas Peninsula 38–9, 92, 103
Akhiropiitos Monastery 136
Antiphonitis Church 136
Apostolos Varnavas 130
Asinou Church (Panayia
 Phorviotissa) 106
Aspros Gorge 40–1
Ayia Moni 107
Ayia Napa 15, 32–3, 64–5
 entertainment 156, 157, 158
 map 32
 monastery 32, 65
 restaurants 169
 walking tour 32–3
Ayia Paraskevi 92
Ayios Ioannis Lampadistis
 Monastery 106–7
Ayios Iraklidhios Monastery 136
Ayios Mamas Monastery 136
Ayios Neophytos 92–3
Ayios Nikolaos of the Cats 78
Ayios Nikolaos tis Stegis 110
Ayios Yeoryios 93

B
banks 185–6
Baths of Aphrodite 96
beaches 15–17, 68–70
Bellapais Abbey 136–7
Besparmak Mountain
 (Pentadaktylos) 9, 151
border crossing
 point 18, 28, 180–1
Buffavento 138
buses 187

C
Camel Trail 142–3
camping 177
Cape Arnouti 144–5
car hire 14, 180
Cedars Valley 148
Chapelle Royale
 (Ayia Ekaterina) 65
children in Cyprus 159, 178
climate 178
Coral Bay 96, 170
credit cards 186
crime 179
customs regulations 179

D
dams 149
disabled travellers 179, 188
driving 14, 179–81, 182

E
embassies and consulates 181
emergency telephone
 numbers 181
Enkomi-Alasia 130
entertainment 156–8

entry formalities 176
Evdhimou Beach 78

F
Famagusta (Gazimagusa)
 21, 58, 120, 122–7, 149
 Ayia Zoni 122
 Ayios Nikolaos 122
 Biddulph's Gate 122
 Carmelite Church 122
 churches of the Templars
 and Hospitallers 125
 Djafer Paşa Baths 122
 Djafer Paşa Fountain 122
 Djamboulat Museum 122
 entertainment 158
 Lala Mustafa Paşa Mosque 122–3
 Medrese 123
 Nestorian Church 124
 Othello's Tower 124
 restaurants 170
 shopping 155
 Sinan Paşa Mosque 124
 St George of the Greeks 124–5
 St George of the Latins 125
 Tanner's Mosque 125
 Venetian Palace and Namik
 Kemal Prison 125
 Venetian Walls 126
ferry services 177
Fontana Amorosa 97
food and drink
 eating out 166–71
 shopping for 154

G
Governor's Beach 78
Grivas Museum 97
Guzelyurt Bay 151

H
Hala Sultan Tekke (Tekke of
 Umm Haram) 65
health matters 182
hitch hiking 182

I
insurance 180, 182–3

K
Kakopetria 110
Kalopanayiotis 111
Kantara Castle 131
Karpas (Kirpasa) Peninsula
 9, 103, 121, 131, 151
Kato Pyrgos 150
Khirokitia 78–9
Khrysorroyiatissa Monastery 111
Kiti Tower 66
Kolossi Castle 79
Kourion (Curium) 80–1, 158
Kourion Museum 82
Kykko Monastery 109, 112
Kyrenia (Girne) 21, 134–5
 castle 134–5
 Decorative Arts Museum 134
 entertainment 156, 158
 Folk Art Museum 134
 Kyrenia ship 135

Lusignan Towers 135–6
 restaurants 171
 shopping 155
Kyrenia Hills 9, 120

L
Lady's Mile Beach 82
Lambousa 138
language 21,183–4
Lara Bay 97, 116, 148
Larnaca 30–1, 58–63
 Archaeological Museum 62
 Ayios Lazaros 31, 61
 entertainment 157
 fort 30, 62
 Kamares (Aqueduct) 62
 Kimon the Athenian 30–1
 Kition 60–1
 Pierides Museum 31, 63
 restaurants 169
 shopping 153
 walking tour 30–1
 Zeno the Stoic 63
Lefka 138
Lefkara 13, 82–3, 154
Limassol 34–5, 72–5
 Amathus 74
 Archaeological Museum 75
 castle (Cyprus Medieval
 Museum) 35, 74–5
 entertainment 158
 Folk Art Museum 74
 restaurants 170
 shopping 153
 walking tour 34–5
 zoo and gardens 35, 75
local time 190
lost property 184

M
Makheras Monastery 112–13
Marion 97
measurements and sizes 184–5
media 185
medical treatment 182
Mesaoria Plain 9, 120
money 185–186
Mount Olympus 15, 114

N
national holidays 186
Nicosia 20, 21, 24–9, 44–57, 103
 Arabahmet Mosque 52
 Archangel Gabriel
 Monastery 46
 Archbishop's Palace 27, 46
 Atatürk Meydani 29
 Ayios Ioannis 27, 46–7
 Ayios Lazaros 31
 Bedesten 52
 border crossing point
 18, 28, 181–2
 Büyük Haman (Turkish
 Baths) 29, 52
 Büyük Han 29, 52–3
 Byzantine Museum 27, 47
 Cyprus (Archaeological)
 Museum 25, 47
 Dervish Paşa Konagi 53

entertainment   156, 157, 158
Famagusta Gate   27, 48
Folk Art Museum   48
Greek Nicosia   24–7, 46–51
Hadjigeorgakis Kornessios
House   27, 48
Handicraft Centre   48, 153
Kumarcilar Hani   29, 54
Kykko Metochi   49
Kyrenia (Girne) Gate   28, 54
Laiki Yitonia   24, 49, 152
Lapidary Museum   29, 54
Latin Archbishopric   55
Leventis Museum   24, 50
Library of Sultan
Mahmut II   55
Mevlevi Tekke (Turkish
Ethnographic Museum)   28, 55
municipal gardens   25, 50
Museum of Barbarism   56
National Struggle
Museum   27, 51
Omerye Mosque   26, 51
Paphos Gate   25, 51
Presidential Palace   51
restaurants   168–9, 170
Selimiye Mosque   29, 56–7
shopping   25, 152–3, 155
Turkish Nicosia   52–7
Venetian walls   27, 51
walking tours   24–7, 28–9
Nissi Beach   66

O
opening times   187
organised tours   187

P
Palea Paphos   98–9
Panayia Angeloktisti   67

Panayia Eleousa   114
Panayia Khryseleousa   100
Panayia Theotokos   114
Panayia tou Araka   114
Pano Panayia (Birthplace of
Makarios)   114–5
Paphos   20, 36–7, 84, 86–7, 90–1
Archaeological Museum   87
Ayia Kyriaki   86
Ayia Solomoni and Ayios
Lamprianos Catacombs   86
Byzantine castle   86
Byzantine Museum   86–7
entertainment   156–8
Ethnographical Museum   87
fort   36, 90
mosaics (House of Dionysos,
Theseus and Aion)   37, 90–1
Odeion   37, 91
restaurants   168
Saranta Kolones   37
shopping   154
St Paul's Pillar   37, 86
Tombs of the Kings   91
walking tour   36–7
Papousta   150
Paralimni   67
Peristerona Church   115
Petra tou Romiou   100
Peyia   100
pharmacies   187
Phikardhou   103, 118
photography   187
Pissouri   83
places of worhsip   181, 188
Platres   118
police   188
Polis   20, 100–1, 171
Pomos Point   150
post offices   188

Protaras (Fig Tree Bay)
                               70, 157, 170
public transport   188–9

S
Salamis   132–3, 171
Salt Lake   70
Sanctuary of Apollo   83
senior citizens   189
shopping   152–5
Soli   140
sport   160–5
St Hilarion   139
Stavros tou Ayiasmati   119
Stavrovouni   70
student and youth travel   189

T
Tamassos   119
taxis   189
telephones   189
Throni   119
tipping   190
toilets   190
tourist offices   190
travelling in Cyprus   176
Troodhitissa Monastery   119
Troodos Mountains
                        8, 15, 42–3, 104–19

V
voltage   181
Vouni Palace   141

W
wine villages   150

Y
Yeroskipos   101, 154
Yeroskipos Folk Museum   101

ACKNOWLEDGEMENTS
The Automobile Association wishes to thank the following photographers and libraries for their assistance in the preparation of this book.

MALCOLM BIRKITT took all the photographs in this book (AA PHOTO LIBRARY) except for:
J ALLAN CASH PHOTOLIBRARY p94 Bride & Groom, p118 Pano Platres, p130 View from Kantara Castle, p133 Roman Gymnasium, p162 Dhassoudi Beach
ROBERT BULMER p39 View to Cadearnaouti, p41 Aspros Gorge, p102 Akamas Shore, p143 Camel Trail, p144 Cape Arnouti, p145 Cape Arnouti, p151 Sandy Bay on Karpas Peninsular, p154 Nicosia Market
INTERNATIONAL PHOTOBANK Front Cover Paphos
LIFE FILE PHOTOGRAPHIC LIBRARY p126 Lion of St Mark
NATURE PHOTOGRAPHERS LTD p102 Cyprus Moufflon (Michael Gore), Loggerhead Turtle (J Sutherland), p117 Cyprus Warbler (Michael Gore)
SPECTRUM COLOUR LIBRARY p125 St George of the Greeks, p127 City Walls, Famagusta, p131 Kantara Castle, p138 Buffavento Castle
The remaining photographs are held in the AA PHOTO LIBRARY with contributions from:
Robert Bulmer, Roy Rainford